To Reub.

D0054444

yourself -
and God.

mom

(May 2012)

1 Minute a Day
Copyright © 2008 by David Jeremiah

Published in Nashville, Tennessee, by Thomas Nelson.
Thomas Nelson is a registered trademark of Thomas Nelson, Inc

Published in association with Yates & Yates, LLP,
Attorneys and Literary Agents, Orange, CA.

Special thanks to William Kruidenier for assistance in writing *1 Minute A Day*.

Thomas Nelson, Inc. titles may be purchased in bulk for educational,
business, fund-raising, or sales promotional use. For information,
please e-mail SpecialMarkets@ThomasNelson.com.

Unless otherwise noted, all Scripture references are from
The Holy Bible, New King James Version ©1979, 1980,
1982, 1992, Thomas Nelson, Inc.

Other Scripture references are taken from *The Holy Bible,
New International Version* (NIV) © 1984 by the International
Bible Society. Used by permission of Zondervan Bible Publishers.

Project Manager: Lisa Stilwell
Designed by ThinkPen Design, Inc., www.thinkpendesign.com

ISBN-10: 1–4041–8726–X
ISBN-13: 978–1–4041–8726–9

Printed and bound in Canada

www.thomasnelson.com

DAVID JEREMIAH

1 minute a day

Instant Inspiration for the Busy Life

THOMAS NELSON
Since 1798

NASHVILLE   DALLAS   MEXICO CITY   RIO DE JANEIRO   BEIJING

One thing I do,
forgetting those things
which are behind and reaching
forward to those things which are
ahead, I press toward the goal
for the prize of the upward call
of God in Christ Jesus.

PHILIPPIANS 3:13–14

Table of Contents

58 Defenses	**70** Peer Pressure	**82** Communication	**94** Gratitude
59 Fear	**71** God	**83** Heavenly Treasures	**95** Starting Over
60 Stewardship of Health	**72** Money	**84** Not of the World	**96** God's Voice
61 Confession	**73** Hope	**85** Redeem the Time	**97** Love for God
62 Grace	**74** Expectation	**86** God's Omnipotence	**98** God's Work
63 The Bible	**75** Speech	**87** Truth	**99** Influence
64 Assurance	**76** Signs from God	**88** Appreciation	**100** Generous Living
65 Purpose	**77** Slow to Speak	**89** Sowing & Reaping	**101** Knowledge of God's Word
66 Life Choices	**78** Understanding	**90** Perfectionism	**102** Discipline (Training)
67 Conversion	**79** The Glory of Man	**91** God's Calling	**103** Gratification
68 Opinions	**80** Accomplishment	**92** Abundant Giving	**104** Relationships
69 Second Coming	**81** Courage	**93** Resistance	**105** Unfaithfulness

| 106 | 118 | 131 | 144 |
| The Cross | Wisdom | Anger | Despair |

| 107 | 119 | 132 | 145 |
| Education | Wholeness | Loneliness | Tragedy |

| 108 | 120 | 133 | 146 |
| Jesus | Grief | Time and Eternity | God's Guidance |

| 109 | 121 | 134 | 147 |
| Miracles | Service | Temptation | Pessimism |

| 110 | 122 | 135 | 148 |
| The Devil | Church | Endurance | Balance |

| 111 | 123 | 136 | 149 |
| Religion | Personal Peace | Spiritual Deafness | Gossip |

| 112 | 124 | 137 | 150 |
| Self-Protection | Compassion | Converting | Christlikeness |

| 113 | 125 | 138 | 151 |
| Cheating | Success | Impartiality | Paradoxes |

| 114 | 126 | 139 | 152 |
| Disappointment | Trust | Holiness | Authority |

| 115 | 127 | 140 | 153 |
| Singleness | Pride | Mercy | Optimism |

| 116 | 128 | 141 | 154 |
| Friendships | Purposeful Living | Parenting | Honesty |

| 117 | 129 | 142 | 155 |
| Self-Acceptance | Pain | God's Forgiveness | Values Clarification |

| 130 | 143 |
| Discouragement | Choices |

LIFE IN THE FAST LANE!

Jesus said, "I have come that they may have life, and that they may have it more abundantly" (John 10:10). No question about it: God wants us to enjoy an over-the-top life, in which we live each day to the fullest, making the most of every single minute.

But sometimes our days become so intense that we lose sight of what really matters. We rush here and there without a feeling of meaning or spiritual connection—it's all just a blur.

I hope that the *1 Minute a Day* thoughts in this book will give you just a quick shot of God's energy and vigor. They're not a substitute for your regular Bible reading, of course—they're more like a protein bar than a square meal. But I hope they remind you of God's plan and purpose for your life and help you reconnect with your goal of loving and serving God better in the midst of the daily rush.

It seems that we're all running these days. Let's make sure we're running in the right direction.

David Jeremiah

Health

Everywhere you go these days, human health is a hot topic. Organically grown food, nutritional supplements, exercise, alternative therapies—you need to be strong just to keep up! But that's okay—we need to learn to be good stewards of our physical health.

But did you know we also need to be "heart healthy"? By that I mean spiritually and emotionally strong. Experts are learning that human health is a rope of three strands: body, soul, and spirit. And the Bible gives us direction for how to keep all three strands vibrant and strong. The healthiest bodies are those with healthy hearts.

Eat right and exercise, but make sure you don't neglect your soul.

The righteousness of Your testimonies is everlasting; Give me understanding, and I shall live.
PSALM 119:144

Materialism

Consider these three parts of our culture: garage sales, mini-storage facilities, and landfills. They're all signs that we've got more "stuff" than we know what to do with! Everyone struggles with saying "Enough!" when it comes to material things.

Finding the balance between greed and contentment is a challenge. And there are no rule books to tell us when enough is enough—not even the Bible. Like human fathers, God lets His children wrestle with some decisions—like how much stuff to own. But He does give us principles in His Word, along with the promise of guidance from His Spirit.

Talk to God about the best use of your material resources. With His help, you'll be well on your way to a healthy, balanced life.

"Consider the lilies of the field, how they grow: they neither toil nor spin; and yet I say to you that even Solomon in all his glory was not arrayed like one of these. Now if God so clothes the grass of the field, which today is, and tomorrow is thrown into the oven, will He not much more clothe you, O you of little faith?"

MATTHEW 6:28–30

Dangers, Toils, and Snares

In his wonderful hymn "Amazing Grace," John Newton wrote these famous words: "Through many dangers, toils, and snares we have already come." And John Newton knew whereof he wrote! He was a man who had escaped death a dozen times or more before his life was changed forever by God's amazing grace.

Each of us, if we stop and examine our lives in detail, can identify times when we went through "dangers, toils, and snares." And that's the point—we went "through"! Too often we are rescued or saved from calamity without looking back and giving God credit for His amazing grace that carried us through.

Take a minute today to think about all God has brought you through. Reflecting on His grace in the past will give you new confidence for the present and future.

Yet in all these things we are more than conquerors through Him who loved us.
ROMANS 8:37

Promises

If there's one thing most people don't like about the modern political process, it would have to be the abundance of promises candidates make, but often can't keep. After they are elected, the political process gets so complicated it becomes impossible for politicians to keep all their campaign promises.

But promises are important—and not just in politics. We depend on the ability to trust one another's words in order to have meaningful relationships in life. The Bible tells us that God's words are wholly trustworthy—that they last forever. Whatever God says, whatever promises He makes, we know His words will never fail.

An absolutely perfect promise keeper—that's the kind of God He is!

Let us hold fast the confession of our hope without wavering, for He who promised is faithful.

HEBREWS 10:23

Destiny

These profound words, attributed to English novelist Charles Reade, serve as an important reminder of the power of little things: "Sow an act, and you reap a habit. Sow a habit, and you reap a character. Sow a character, and you reap a destiny."[1] It's easy to lose the connection between actions and destiny. In between are habits and character, the stuff of which lifetimes are made and destinies realized.

Today you and I will act a hundred times. We would do well to remember the Bible's words that "the steps of a good man are ordered by the LORD" (Psalm 37:23). Don't lose sight of the connection between today's acts and tomorrow's destiny.

God has a wonderful plan for you. Embrace every minute of it by acting thoughtfully and diligently.

We also glory in tribulations, knowing that tribulation produces perseverance; and perseverance, character; and character, hope.

ROMANS 5:3–4

God's Truth

Albert Einstein, the famous physicist, explained relativity this way: When a man sits with a pretty girl for an hour, it seems like a minute. But when he sits on a hot stove for a minute, it seems like an hour. That's relativity, he said.[2]

Lots of things in life are relative—they change when compared to something else. But one thing that is not relative is God's truth found in the Bible. The words of Scripture were true when they were written, are true today, and will be true when we're long gone. We can safely build our lives on the unchanging foundation of Scripture.

If you're looking for unfailing truth, look in God's Word.

The law of the LORD is perfect,
converting the soul;
The testimony of the LORD is sure,
making wise the simple.
PSALM 19:7

Procrastination

There's something I've been putting off for too long: trying to figure out why we put things off. And I think I've figured it out: we procrastinate because we don't value every moment and every action as highly as God values them.

Everything is sacred to God. Sure, some things are more important than others in the long run. But that doesn't mean those lesser things are without value in God's sight. Therefore, they ought to be accomplished. The Bible introduces us to a God who is the Creator of all and Lord of all—and who accomplishes everything at just the right time.

Let God show you His concern for even the smallest details of your life, and let Him fill you with His motivation.

 He has made everything beautiful in its time.
ECCLESIASTES 3:11

Adversity

Inspiration can strike anywhere—even in a cancer ward. A German software engineer had a brainstorm while taking treatment for leukemia and now owns a company based on the idea he had. It just goes to show that adversity can be the beginning, not the end, of the road.

If you're facing adversity right now, do you think it's a dead end, or are you looking for what God might want to show you? The Bible is a book written to people in trouble—the whole human race! Open its pages and open your eyes. God may be trying to show you something new.

May you experience His comfort during troubled times, as well as His power to create miracles even out of the bleakest circumstances.

He who heeds the word wisely will find good,
And whoever trusts in the LORD,
happy is he.

PROVERBS 16:20

Future

It happens to every parent: your first child leaves the nest to begin her first day of school. What will the future hold? And then the day comes when you watch your last child graduate from college. Again, what will the future hold? Life is filled with fearful moments that present questions for which we have no answers.

But what the future holds is really not the question. What really matters is Who holds the future. In the Bible, God promises that He will never leave us nor forsake us. That promise, and a thousand others from His Word, gives us the answers to our questions about the future.

The next time you find yourself wondering what the future will hold, take a minute to fill your mind with God's promises, and remember that you're not walking into the future alone.

 "I am with you always, even to the end of the age."
MATTHEW 28:20

Envy

I've heard it said that some ulcers are caused by inflammation of the "wishbone." And I can believe it. Envy is a robber of happiness and destroyer of relationships. When we start turning green with envy, we are ripe for trouble.

The Bible's solution to envy is three words: "Love your neighbor." But that simple advice is harder to implement than it sounds. Living free from envy and jealousy seems beyond us at times. But it's not beyond God. In the Bible, you'll discover how God can love others through you. You can enjoy life by living free of envy—and ulcers!

Let God teach you to take pleasure in others' success, and celebrate the blessings of your own life.

 Beloved, let us love one another, for love is of God; and everyone who loves is born of God and knows God.
1 JOHN 4:7

Satisfaction

In 1965, a famous band of British musicians proclaimed to the world, "I can't get no satisfaction"—and more than forty years later, they're still singing the same song by that very title.[3] That must say something about how elusive satisfaction is. Everyone's busy, everyone's searching—but how many are truly satisfied with life?

Where should we look for satisfaction? Inwardly, by being perfect? Or outwardly, by acquiring the world's symbols of success? A man in the Old Testament declared that he would be satisfied with just one thing: to live all his life in God's presence. You can read his words in Psalm 27.

Reach for your Bible and discover the secret to true contentment: a life filled with God's grace and love.

Whatever was to my profit I now consider loss for the sake of Christ. What is more, I consider everything a loss compared to the surpassing greatness of knowing Christ Jesus my Lord.
PHILIPPIANS 3:7–8 NIV

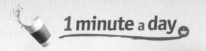

Time

No one can add to it, no one can take away from it, no one can stop its advance, and every single person has exactly the same amount of it. What is this mysterious thing? It's that evasive, fleeting entity called time.

Twenty-four hours a day, 168 hours per week, 8,760 hours per year—that seems like a lot of time. Yet how often do we say, "Sorry, I just don't have time"? We need to pray what a man in the Old Testament prayed: Lord, teach us to number our days—to use our time wisely (Psalm 90:12).

With God's help, you can live as a good steward of your time and enjoy a rich, abundant life.

 See then that you walk circumspectly, not as fools but as wise, redeeming the time, because the days are evil. Therefore do not be unwise, but understand what the will of the Lord is.
EPHESIANS 5:15–17

Guidance

Have you seen the navigation devices available in new cars, or as add-ons for older models? I was given one of these gizmos as a gift, and it is certainly helpful—though I can still manage to get lost.

Wouldn't it be nice if we had a device to guide us through the twists and turns of everyday life? While that tool doesn't exist, here's something even better: a Book to guide you and access to the Author for personal advice. The Bible and its Author can't keep me from getting lost while driving, but they have kept me from getting lost in life.

Take time to familiarize yourself with God's Guidebook. It will be an indispensable guide for the rest of your life.

Your ears shall hear a word behind you, saying,
"This is the way, walk in it,"
Whenever you turn to the right hand
Or whenever you turn to the left.
ISAIAH 30:21

Attitude of Gratitude

Did you hear about the man who gave up his seat on the bus to a woman? She was so surprised, she fainted. When she came to, she thanked the man—and he fainted!

Sometimes it takes an exaggeration to make a point, doesn't it? Simple expressions of gratitude, appreciation, and thankfulness are so rare that they shock us when we experience them.

We all can find things to be grateful for. Someone once said, "If you can't be thankful for what you have, be thankful for what you've escaped."[4] The Bible has a simple admonition on this point: give thanks in all things.

Gratitude is a great attitude to develop. It makes us more content, more generous, and more in touch with the God who abundantly blesses us.

Develop an attitude of gratitude starting today.

 Oh, give thanks to the LORD, for He is good!
For His mercy endures forever.
Let the redeemed of the LORD say so,
Whom He has redeemed from the hand of the enemy.
PSALM 107:1–2

Love

Those of you who remember the turbulent 1960s will recall seeing the word *love* spelled L-U-V. That spelling stood for the "groovy kind of love" that was supposed to reshape the world. Fortunately, luv is now relegated to texters.

Another spelling of love has stood the test of time: G-I-V-E. The Bible says that God so loved the world that He gave. . . . Love, in its purest form, is an action. When we give to others what is most valuable to ourselves, we prove our love.

Looking for a great love story? Read the Gospel of John in the New Testament and discover God's love language.

In this is love, not that we loved God, but that He loved us and sent His Son to be the propitiation for our sins.

1 JOHN 4:10

Perseverance

Almost everyone is familiar with the story of Thomas Edison and the lightbulb, how he tried nearly a thousand times to perfect it before succeeding. With that kind of perseverance, failure isn't an option. Each trial simply eliminates one obstacle to success until all the obstacles have been removed.

Is there a goal you've given up on because you've failed many times in the past? I encourage you to use the Edison approach and refuse to be defeated until you achieve success. The Bible teaches that God can use failure as a side door to success if we will just stay the course.

Don't give up! Success might be just around the corner.

Let patience have its perfect work, that you may be perfect and complete, lacking nothing.
JAMES 1:4

Selfishness

In his book *My Personal Best,* legendary UCLA basketball coach John Wooden wrote that selfishness is a character flaw. Not a trait, but a flaw. Wooden wanted most of UCLA's points to come as a result of passing because it worked against the tendency toward selfishness.[5]

I think we tend to be selfish because we're insecure about the future. Like squirrels in the summer, we tend to hoard our acorns as if there will never be any more. But if we take the Bible's perspective, we will open our hands so that God is free to fill them whenever we have a need.

We can trust God to provide for us. We don't need to grab and grasp, looking at others with suspicion. We can look to the interests of others because we know God is looking out for us.

Instead of a life of selfishness, develop a life of selflessness.

Our soul waits for the LORD;
He is our help and our shield.
For our heart shall rejoice in Him,
Because we have trusted in His holy name.
PSALM 33:20–21

Poverty

I have heard poverty in the ancient world described this way: a poor person was one who was faced at the beginning of the day with the task of finding food for that day. By that measure, most of us would be considered fabulously wealthy!

Unfortunately, there are many in our world who must begin each day with the task of finding food. God wants to meet their needs, and wants to do it through those He has blessed with an abundance. The Bible is full of reasons and ways to give encouragement to those struggling to make ends meet.

God is tenderhearted toward the poor and downtrodden. Look for opportunities to share with others the blessings God has bestowed on you. That is one of the best—and most rewarding—ways to please God.

 The generous soul will be made rich,
And he who waters will also be watered himself.
PROVERBS 11:25

Bitterness

People in some parts of the world live in constant fear of a volcano erupting. The hot gases and lava that eventually spew forth can wreak havoc for miles around. Fortunately, there are always warning signs that an eruption is imminent.

The human heart can sometimes act like a volcano—but it often erupts without any warning at all, and people get hurt. Natural volcanoes can't be stopped, but human volcanoes can—by letting go of bitterness before it erupts. The Bible is God's textbook on defusing bitterness through forgiveness. When we remember how much we have been forgiven, we find it easier to share that grace with others.

Instead of exploding, try forgiving. You and those around you will be glad you did.

 Let all bitterness, wrath, anger, clamor, and evil speaking be put away from you, with all malice. And be kind to one another, tenderhearted, forgiving one another, even as God in Christ forgave you.
EPHESIANS 4:31–32

Restoration

Anyone who has restored an old piece of furniture knows it's a lot of work: put on the rubber gloves, pour on the chemicals, scrape off the four coats of paint, sand it down, stain it, varnish it—after several weeks, you have a piece of furniture that is ready to be used again.

Restoring relationships takes hard work as well. Approaching, talking, confessing, forgiving—it's not easy. Removing the resentment, hurt, and distrust restores a damaged relationship to its original glory. The Bible says to do whatever it takes to be restored to one another. It's a word to the wise.

Fortunately for us, we have the ultimate model of reconciliation: God sending His Son so that we might be forgiven and have a restored relationship with Him. Let's follow God's example by being quick to make the first move toward reconciliation.

Be kindly affectionate to one another with brotherly love, in honor giving preference to one another; . . . Do not be overcome by evil, but overcome evil with good.
ROMANS 12:10, 21

Revenge

Here's a new word for you: *revengeology,* the fine art of payback. It's the latest twist on the old bromide, "Don't get mad, get even." I have to tell you, there's a problem with getting even: it's a never-ending cycle of hurt.

Here's another problem with vengeance: it makes you prosecutor, judge, jury, and executioner—roles to which none of us has been appointed. In the Bible, God says, "Vengeance is Mine, I will repay" (Romans 12:19). And He will, in His good time. Why waste energy and creativity on vengeance when it could be invested in love—say, loving your enemy?

Don't let wounds fester. Releasing them to the Lord—not stewing and retaliating—is the only way to break the hold they have on you.

If your enemy is hungry, give him bread to eat;
And if he is thirsty, give him water to drink;
For so you will heap coals of fire on his head,
And the LORD will reward you.
PROVERBS 25:21–22

Making Plans

Do you plan every detail of your life, or do you take the "whatever will be, will be" approach? Some people think their plans control the future, while others believe the future has already been planned. The truth is probably somewhere in between.

I've noticed that people in the Bible weren't afraid to plan—but they also had a healthy regard for God's "master plan." One verse strikes a good balance. Paraphrased, it says, "We make plans, trusting God to guide our steps" (Proverbs 16:9). Planning diligently while remaining flexible seems like a good approach. That way, we take an active role in our future, while remaining dependent on God's plans and provision.

Plan today to discover what the Bible says about the benefits of planning. There's no greater guide to preparing for the future.

Unless the LORD builds the house,
They labor in vain who build it.
PSALM 127:1

Unfulfilled Dreams

Almost everyone has heard the speech Dr. Martin Luther King Jr. gave in Washington, D.C., in 1963. In that speech, he declared over and over, "I have a dream." Sadly, his dream became a nightmare when his life was cut short. But his dream continues to move America toward the reality of racial equality.

When dreams are cut short, we are faced with two choices: retreat into disappointment and despair, or rise up and dream again. Any dream worth dreaming once is worth dreaming two, three, or a hundred times. Biblical prophets dreamed big dreams—and so can you!

Keep dreaming, and keep listening for God's voice and calling on your life. Know that He has good plans for you and is able to make your dreams come true.

 " 'And it shall come to pass in the last days, says God,
That I will pour out of My Spirit on all flesh;
Your sons and your daughters shall prophesy,
Your young men shall see visions,
Your old men shall dream dreams.' "
ACTS 2:17

Moral Boundaries

A funny thing happens when researchers take little kids to a huge, open field with lots of room to play. They are hesitant and unsure of themselves. But when given a fenced-in area to enjoy, they relax and play without a care in the world.

What's the difference? Boundaries. When we know where the boundaries are in life, what the rules are, we are more confident and less fearful. Boundaries allow us to relate to the world. The Bible contains God's boundaries, the areas within which we can do what we were created to do: work, play, and have a ball!

Take time to get to know God's boundaries, knowing that they were placed there for your protection and good.

 "Take My yoke upon you and learn from Me, for I am gentle and lowly in heart, and you will find rest for your souls."
MATTHEW 11:29

Brokenness

A few generations ago, if something broke, it was fixed. Today, we live in a throw-away world where things are designed to be replaced when they break.

That's okay for toasters and hair dryers, but it doesn't work too well with the human heart. When your heart breaks, you can't go to the big-box discount store and get a new one. Fortunately, broken hearts can be put together again—but it takes God to do it, the Bible says. He's the only one with the power to restore us when we've been hurt.

If your heart is broken, don't discard it. Let God take a look. It may take a little time and trust, but rest assured that He's never seen one yet He couldn't mend.

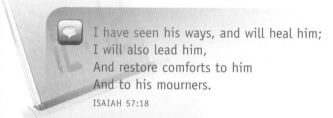

I have seen his ways, and will heal him;
I will also lead him,
And restore comforts to him
And to his mourners.
ISAIAH 57:18

Expectations

A lot of people today—especially single people looking for a life partner—choose to set their sights, and often their standards, really low. They're afraid if they have high expectations and things don't work out, they'll be crushed with disappointment.

But who wants to go through life not hoping for the best, not striving to be a high achiever? Can I share a secret I've learned that helps me avoid disappointment? Instead of putting my confidence in people—including myself—I put it in God. The Bible is filled with His promises to me, and I've never been disappointed with a single one.

Set your sights high. No matter what happens, you're in the care of a mighty God.

Trust in the LORD with all your heart,
And lean not on your own understanding;
In all your ways acknowledge Him,
And He shall direct your paths.
PROVERBS 3:5–6

Conflict

When the charter of the United Nations was signed in October 1945, its stated purposes were to maintain peace and security, solve problems, and promote harmony among nations. Since 1945, however, there have been only twenty-six days when there was not an armed conflict somewhere in the world.

But let's not blame nations alone. How many days have you gone without a conflict of some sort—large or small—between you and another person? Given the human propensity for conflict, it's no wonder the Old Testament prophets looked forward to the coming of the Prince of Peace.

We're all thirsty for the lasting world peace we don't experience here on earth. But with God's help, we can find personal peace and in turn become peacemakers in the world around us.

But now in Christ Jesus you who once were far off have been brought near by the blood of Christ. For He Himself is our peace, who has made both one, and has broken down the middle wall of separation.
EPHESIANS 2:13–14

Undeserved Gifts

Most of what we receive in this life is deserved. We deserve a bonus at our job because we worked hard, or we deserve a first-place finish in a race because of all the grueling workouts we put in. We have a word for things we receive but don't necessarily deserve: gifts.

Christmas gifts, birthday gifts, unexpected gifts—they fall into the category of what the Bible calls grace: things we receive that we don't earn. And when you add them up, the list of God's gifts is long: love, forgiveness, and countless blessings. The Bible tells us that God gives because He loves. That's the nature of grace: receiving without deserving.

Pause for a second to thank God for the undeserved blessings He has poured into your life—a moment to connect with the One who has shown you grace is well worth the time.

 For by grace you have been saved through faith, and that not of yourselves; it is the gift of God, not of works, lest anyone should boast.
EPHESIANS 2:8–9

Reconciliation

Think of all the people in the world who do not live in peace: there are Jews and Palestinians, North Koreans and South Koreans, Iraqi insurgents and Iraqi nationalists. But there are also friends, relatives, and marriage partners who live lives of estrangement. To close the wounds that separate means to be reconciled. And to be reconciled, someone has to take a first step and extend a hand.

The Bible says we were separated from God but can now be reconciled to Him because He took the first step. That's really the story of the whole Bible—God extending His hand to us. Thanks to His amazing grace, we enjoy a restored relationship with Him and, according to Scripture, have received "the ministry of reconciliation" to share His grace with others (2 Corinthians 5:18).

The Bible tells us that blessed are the peacemakers. Let's look for ways to be peacemakers, beginning with a word of thanks to God for His gracious reconciliation.

Now thanks be to God who always leads us in triumph in Christ, and through us diffuses the fragrance of His knowledge in every place.

2 CORINTHIANS 2:14

Value

You can tell how much I value something by the effort I put into finding it. If I lose a paper clip on my desk, I only look for a second before grabbing another one. But if I lose my wallet, I won't rest until it's recovered.

Did you know there's a way to measure how much God values us? The Bible says He loves us so much that He sent His only Son to earth to find us. Think of that—God giving His Son because you and I were lost. Nothing makes me feel so valuable as knowing what God did to find me.

God values you, too, more than you might realize. Remember He would have sent His Son to the cross even if you were the only person on earth. Wow! Amazing love.

 The Son of Man has come to seek and to save that which was lost.
LUKE 19:10

Redemption

As someone who flies often, I am very familiar with the "frequent flyer" plans of most airlines. When I exchange frequent flyer miles for an airline ticket, I tell the clerk I want to redeem my miles. To redeem something means to turn in one thing and get another in exchange.

Redemption is a familiar word to Bible readers. In ancient times, slaves were redeemed from servitude when someone exchanged money for their freedom. Likewise, God redeemed us by exchanging the life of His Son for our freedom from the marketplace of sin. It was costly for God, but liberating for us.

The Bible speaks often about the freedom we experience in our new life in Christ. Do not forget that your freedom came with a price, a price paid out of God's great love.

 God has given us eternal life, and this life is in His Son.
1 JOHN 5:11

Shame

Sometimes I shudder just thinking about it—that feeling of being ashamed. The dictionary says *shame* is a "painful emotion caused by consciousness of guilt, shortcoming, or impropriety."[6] And it is painful, especially the shame that comes after we've done something we know we shouldn't have.

Some people avoid the pain of shame by suppressing their sense of right and wrong, by ignoring their conscience. Instead, why not let shame be a teacher that leads us to God and His forgiveness? The pain of shame can do something else: it can motivate us to avoid experiencing that same pain again in the future.

No one enjoys the feeling of shame, but put it to work for you. Let it drive you into God's loving arms of forgiveness, and let the memory of it keep you on the right path.

 If we confess our sins, He is faithful and just to forgive us our sins and to cleanse us from all unrighteousness.
1 JOHN 1:9

Celebration

Who doesn't like a great party? Cities celebrate their sports teams, families celebrate a grandfather turning one hundred, and individuals celebrate losing those extra ten pounds. Those are great reasons to celebrate. But have you ever been invited to a party for a person who apologized for doing something wrong?

There's a story in the Bible of a giant party held for a young man who decided to start living a better life. Jesus told that story to show the kinds of things God celebrates. Maybe no one's ever thrown a party for you when you turned over a new leaf—but I'm sure God did. He rejoices in your victories, large and small.

When we turn our lives toward Him, we bring God joy. Have you given Him a reason to celebrate today?

There will be more joy in heaven over one sinner who repents than over ninety-nine just persons who need no repentance.

LUKE 15:7

Amazing Grace

A company that provides Internet access to the public recently sued one of its customers for sending out millions of spam e-mails. The Internet company won the suit, and the individual was ordered to pay $11.2 billion—that's "billion" with a *b*—in damages. Needless to say, that was a judgment he was unable to pay.

I know what it feels like to have a judgment I could never, ever pay. It's the debt I owe for sinning against a holy God. Fortunately, the Bible says that the same God who issued the judgment also paid the fine by sending His Son to pay what I could never afford.

That kind of grace is almost unfathomable, and it calls us to live a life of gratitude to such a great Giver. In the words of songwriter Isaac Watts, "Love so amazing, so divine demands my soul, my life, my all."

 And He said to me, "My grace is sufficient for you, for My strength is made perfect in weakness."
2 CORINTHIANS 12:9

Opportunity

Businessmen discuss "opportunity costs" when they decide the costs of a certain course of action. If we invest over "here," they say, the cost will be the lost opportunity to invest over "there." Every decision has a cost—the cost of lost opportunity.

There is a story in the New Testament about a man who spent his life building barns to store up his accumulating wealth. The opportunity cost to him was the loss of time to attend to his soul—a hefty price to pay for gathering up worldly wealth.

Full barns are great so long as they don't result in an empty soul. Make sure you don't miss out on the kingdom in your pursuit of the things of this world.

For whoever desires to save his life will lose it, but whoever loses his life for My sake will find it. For what profit is it to a man if he gains the whole world, and loses his own soul?

MATTHEW 16:25-26

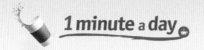

Integrity

In 2005, the Merriam-Webster online dictionary published its list of the words looked up most frequently, and at the top of the list was the word *integrity*. Like many who saw that list, I'm not sure what to make of it. Duke University's Tim Dodd commented, "It's sobering that [people] need to look up integrity in the first place."[7]

Maybe it's a sign that people were really interested in integrity in 2005, which would be a good thing. According to Merriam-Webster, *integrity* refers to "firm adherence to a code of especially moral or artistic values,"[8] something we as a society often lack. But while integrity may vacillate in our world, God's character never does. The Bible says He is the same yesterday, today, and tomorrow —always true and trustworthy.

If you're looking for the true definition of integrity, look no further than God's character as found in the Bible.

For I am the LORD, I do not change.
MALACHI 3:6

Good News

Marvin "Bad News" Barnes was a two-time college All-American basketball player and an ABA All-Star. In 1976 he made it to the NBA, where he lasted only four years. Drugs and alcohol ruined a promising basketball career and landed him in prison, rehab programs, and homelessness. That was the bad news.

The good news is that today, Bad News Barnes is filled with good news. A spiritual awakening and commitment to helping young people has resulted in a new life. His life is like the message of the Bible: the bad news of our failures sets the stage for God's good news in His gospel. The old has passed, the new has come (2 Corinthians 5:17).

If you're seeking that kind of change in your life, God's transformative power is available to you today. He can turn any situation around.

Then I will give them one heart, and I will put a new spirit within them, and take the stony heart out of their flesh, and give them a heart of flesh.
EZEKIEL 11:19

Trouble

Have you seen the new cell phones for children? I cringed when I first heard about this until I learned more. They are designed primarily as a security device—push the "Mom" button and the phone calls Mom, and the same for Dad, 911, and so on.

Children aren't the only ones who need someone to call when they're in trouble. Fortunately, in the Bible we have God's promise: "Call to Me, and I will answer you" (Jeremiah 33:3). And we don't even have to push a button or dial a number!

Cell phones are helpful, but limited. God is an unlimited resource in times of trouble, and He is never out of range There's no adversity He hasn't already seen, no problem He is unable to solve. When you truly seek Him, you will find in Him a refuge and source of incredible strength.

God is our refuge and strength,
A very present help in trouble.
Therefore we will not fear,
Even though the earth be removed.
PSALM 46:1–2

Prayer

For 188 years, the Indiana state legislature began each session with prayer. But a 2005 ruling by a federal judge declared that no prayers could be offered that made overt Christian references. In response, the legislature complied with a "pre-approved prayer" and sought to have the decision overturned. Less than two years later, an appeals court did overturn the ban on using Jesus' name.

One judge remarked, "This victory reminds us and our legislators that we should never surrender one of our most valuable rights. . ."[9]

The Bible confirms that legislative ruling—God invites us to pray to Him in Jesus' name any time and from any place. He also promises that those who seek Him will find Him. No circumstance or judicial ruling can separate God from His people.

Prayed Today?

"It shall come to pass
That before they call, I will answer;
And while they are still speaking, I will hear."
ISAIAH 65:24

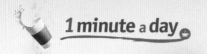
Communion

If you do a search on the Internet for the word communion, almost every link that is returned has a spiritual or religious context. Sometimes *communion* refers to the sacrament of the Lord's Supper, and other times it refers to an organized fellowship of Christian churches.

Communion means oneness, or commonality. The basis for Christians' oneness with each other is the oneness we have with God as individuals. When our fellowship with God is strong, our communion with each other will be sweet. But if we are not in communion with Him, all the rest of our relationships will suffer.

Seek the rich interaction that comes from communing with God and His followers. Sharing the love of God makes our relationships unforgettable.

A new commandment I give to you, that you love one another; as I have loved you, that you also love one another. JOHN 13:34

Strength

Recently a news report featured a three-year-old boy in China who is startling people with his feats of strength. The son of an auto mechanic, this little guy can already lift a car jack that weighs more than eighty pounds.

Muscular strength is important, for sure. But there's another kind of strength that's even more important, and that is moral strength. This kind of inner strength is the ability to do what we should do rather than what we want to do. And often there's a big difference. Fortunately, when God lives in our lives, we have access to His strength.

That indwelling strength gives us the power to resist temptation, overcome challenges, and act selflessly. The next time you're feeling weak, simply let God's strength take over. His power is more than sufficient.

I can do all things through Christ who strengthens me.
PHILIPPIANS 4:13

Fear of the Lord

In C. S. Lewis's *The Lion, the Witch, and the Wardrobe*, Mr. Beaver is telling Lucy about Aslan, the great lion of Narnia. Lucy asks, "Then he isn't safe?" "Safe?" counters Mr. Beaver. "Who said anything about safe? 'Course he isn't safe. But he's good."[10]

Aslan was dangerous and good at the same time—a perfect picture of God. Some people are confused when the Bible says we are to fear the Lord. But to fear God means to stand in awe of God's great power and strength, which He always uses for righteous reasons. Like Aslan of Narnia, God is powerful and gracious at the same time. Though He could easily demolish a mountain, the Bible tells us He will never crush a bruised reed.

We need to respect His mighty power, but we can always trust His perfect love.

Lift up your eyes on high,
And see who has created these things,
Who brings out their host by number;
He calls them all by name,
By the greatness of His might
And the strength of His power;
Not one is missing.
ISAIAH 40:26

Discernment

Do you remember static? Static was what appeared on the television screen in the days before cable or satellite TV when signals were broadcast through the air to an antenna on the roof. Storms, flocks of birds—almost anything could interrupt the signal and cause static on the screen.

Dr. Charles Stanley talks about "spiritual static." That's when our ability to sense God's leading in life gets interrupted by our sin or affection for the things of this world. The Bible says we need discernment—the ability to separate the wise from the foolish in life. That's the only way to maintain a clear signal from God.

Ask God to help you develop discernment, and spend time getting to know His ways of doing things. He will honor your pursuit of wisdom.

The fear of the LORD is the beginning of wisdom; A good understanding have all those who do His commandments. His praise endures forever.
PSALM 111:10

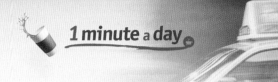

Protection

The famous actor Jimmy Stewart flew twenty combat missions as a squadron leader in World War II. He carried with him a copy of Psalm 91, a gift from his father. Explaining why, he said, "I placed in [God's] hands the squadron I would be leading. . . . I felt myself borne up."[11]

He was referring to Psalm 91's promise that the angels of God will "bear you up" and protect you. Undoubtedly, many soldiers on today's battlefields hold to the same promise. When the going gets tough, we all desperately need a sense of God's presence and power.

Have you asked God to be your protector? Regardless of where your personal battles are, you shouldn't go through them without God's protection.

He who dwells in the secret place of the Most High
Shall abide under the shadow of the Almighty.
I will say of the LORD, "He is my refuge and my fortress;
My God, in Him I will trust."
PSALM 91:1–2

Life

A scientist at Cambridge University in England has been in the news recently for predicting that human life spans will one day approach a thousand years. He believes aging is caused by toxicity in the body. As we learn to reduce the toxins in our body, we will age more slowly and live longer.[12]

Sounds good—but a thousand years? I think I'm going to continue to focus on the Bible's advice about aging. It says, "Teach us to number our days" (Psalm 90:12). Rather than focus on how many days we have, the Bible advises that we live every day to the fullest, enjoying every blessing and benefit God provides.

Quality tends to trump quantity. When we make each day a good day, the number of days we live becomes much less important.

For with You is the fountain of life;
In Your light we see light.
PSALM 36:9

Joy

For most people, happiness works something like a roller coaster. One minute we're on top, surveying the world with satisfaction, and the next minute the bottom drops out and we're headed for the valley below. And that's okay—some days we laugh, and other days we weep.

But I've found through the years that there's something I appreciate even more than happiness. Instead of an emotion, it's a heartfelt foundation—a state of mind called joy. The Bible says that the joy of the Lord can be our strength. So even when the roller coaster rockets for the bottom, we stay on an even keel.

Joy can weather the toughest of storms. Ask God to fill you with the joy of knowing Him and serving Him; and no matter what comes your way, you'll be full of His strength.

 You have filled my heart with greater joy
than when their grain and new wine abound.
PSALM 4:7 NIV

Problems

You may have seen the *Peanuts* comic strip where Linus and Charlie Brown are discussing Linus' philosophy that "There is no problem so big it cannot be run away from."[13] That brings a smile when a kid says it in the comics, but it's definitely not a grown-up way to live.

So what do we do with our problems? Because some of them are like mountains, we just leave them where they are and create new paths around them. But Jesus told His followers that faith could move mountains—and that nothing is impossible for God.

The Bible encourages us to take our problems to Him. When we do, we experience His unbelievable presence, wisdom, and abounding grace.

Cast your burden on the LORD,
And He shall sustain you;
He shall never permit the righteous to be moved.
PSALM 55:22

Self-Control

Here's a piece of American constitutional trivia you may not know. The eighteenth amendment to the United States Constitution banned alcohol as a beverage in America in 1920, but the twenty-first amendment repealed the eighteenth amendment thirteen years later. In other words, the legalized prohibition of alcohol failed.

That grand experiment in legislating morality proved that alcohol is not the primary problem. Nor are guns, sex, or gambling. The problem is a lack of self-control. And the Bible says self-control can't be legislated either.

Fortunately for us, God offers to live in us and control our desires with the power of His indwelling presence for our good and for the good of those around us. When we surrender to His transforming Spirit, we give ourselves the opportunity to become more like Christ.

 But if the Spirit of Him who raised Jesus from the dead dwells in you, He who raised Christ from the dead will also give life to your mortal bodies through His Spirit who dwells in you.

ROMANS 8:11

Defenses

Will anyone ever forget the devastation of Hurricane Katrina in New Orleans and along the Gulf Coast? With the pictures of the destruction still fresh in our minds, the Army Corps of Engineers is working feverishly to shore up the city's defenses against future hurricanes that are bound to come.

We can all learn a valuable spiritual lesson from Hurricane Katrina: we can never let down our guard. The Bible puts it this way: "So, if you think you are standing firm, be careful that you don't fall!" (1 Corinthians 10:12 NIV). The moment we think we can coast, the moment we stop actively guarding ourselves spiritually, that may be the moment we fall victim to the devil's schemes.

The good news is that we can endure tomorrow's storms if we prepare today. Fasting and prayer, memorizing Scripture, developing God-centered relationships—these are all ways we can reinforce our spiritual defenses. Most importantly, of course, we must renew our dependence on God daily. He is the most important shield and fortress in our lives.

Ponder the path of your feet, And let all your ways be established. Do not turn to the right or the left; Remove your foot from evil.

PROVERBS 4:26–27

Fear

Did you know some people have a fear of dust? That's called *amathophobia.* Other people have a fear of stealing—that's called *kleptophobia.* Here's one I know I don't have—*somniphobia,* the fear of sleep. These are funny-sounding words, but what they represent is not funny at all. Fear of any kind is serious business.

In its simplest sense, fear is related to something that might happen, something we can't predict. The Bible makes a simple but profound statement about fear: "Perfect love casts out fear" (1 John 4:18). God's love assures us that whatever happens, He saw it coming and will accomplish His purposes through it. His perfect love always acts for our highest good.

Don't let fear rob you of your joy. Trust His goodness and love for you, and turn over your fears to Him. He is more than able to ease your worries.

 The LORD is my light and my salvation; Whom shall I fear?
PSALM 27:1

Stewardship of Health

I love this sign I saw hanging in an auto repair shop. It said, "If you're smoking in here, you better be on fire!" That sign is typical of the current emphasis in America on helping people to stop smoking. But shouldn't we be just as careful about our health in other areas as well?

Just as our cars were made to run on clean fuel, so were our bodies. They need pure food, clean air, good water, lots of exercise, and peaceful hearts. Our health is a gift from God that we ought to take seriously. It's part of being a good steward of God's grace.

God has given each of us only one body. We need to treat these gifts of God with respect and appreciation.

Do you not know that your body is a temple of the Holy Spirit, who is in you, whom you have received from God? You are not your own; you were bought at a price. Therefore honor God with your body.

1 CORINTHIANS 6:19–20 NIV

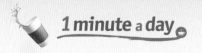

Confession

An older man and his young friend were talking about marriage during their coffee break at work. "It's true," the older one said, "my wife and I do argue occasionally. But we've been committed to never going to bed while angry. 'Course, there was that one time we stayed up for three months straight."

Keeping the communication lines open can be a challenge in the best of marriages. But it's so important—almost as important as maintaining good communication with God. If you make a mistake, just tell Him. It's the only sure way to get a good night's sleep.

When you bring your concerns and mistakes and failures to Him, you'll discover that He is a wonderful listener, and that He was patiently waiting for you . A prayer of confession can lift the heaviest burden from your shoulders and have you sleeping soundly.

 I acknowledged my sin to You,
And my iniquity I have not hidden. . . .
And You forgave the iniquity of my sin.
PSALM 32:5

Grace

The story goes that after losing a tough football game on a Saturday, a famous college coach went to get a haircut on Monday. After a few minutes of silence, the barber said, "Coach, I don't believe I would have played that young quarterback. He cost us the game."

"Well," the coach replied, "if I'd had 'til Monday to think about it, I probably wouldn't have played him either."

Hindsight is always 20/20, isn't it? It's easy for us to be critical of others who make mistakes. Somehow we think we would have done better, even though we make plenty of mistakes ourselves.

I'm so glad God is gracious toward me when I fail! He doesn't rub my mistake in my face; He just helps me back up and encourages me to keep going. He loves me faithfully and continually, and never fails to offer me His grace.

He does the same for you, too!

Through the LORD's mercies we are not consumed,
Because His compassions fail not.
They are new every morning;
Great is Your faithfulness.
LAMENTATIONS 3:22–23

The Bible

When a young family was driving home from church, the father asked his son how he liked the service. "Well," the little boy said, "I liked the singing and the little play they put on. But I thought the commercial was way too long."

In a Hollywood-based culture, it's easy to think of church as entertainment. We sometimes view the preaching of the Bible almost as an interruption. In fact, hearing from God through His Word is central to why Christians gather on Sunday. It may or may not be the most entertaining part of the service, but it is the most important.

The Bible says faith comes by hearing. There's something very powerful about the spoken Word of God. Listen closely the next time you're in church, and you just may hear from God in a fresh new way.

 All Scripture is given by inspiration of God, and is profitable for doctrine, for reproof, for correction, for instruction in righteousness, that the man of God may be complete, thoroughly equipped for every good work.
2 TIMOTHY 3:16–17

Assurance

At a junior college's basketball banquet, the president of the college praised the coach for winning the division championship. Standing next to the president at the podium, the coach asked, "Will you still like me if we don't win next year?"

"Absolutely," the president replied instantly. "I'll still like you. I'll just miss having you around."

Sometimes we think of God as being like that college president—if we don't perform, we had better pack our bags. But nothing could be farther from the truth. The Bible says we are saved and kept by grace, not by our works.

I hope that you have come to know God's promise of assurance. One of the sweetest gifts of His grace is knowing that He will never leave you nor forsake you.

 Let us draw near with a true heart in full assurance of faith, having our hearts sprinkled from an evil conscience and our bodies washed with pure water.
HEBREWS 10:22

Purpose

A classic Calvin and Hobbes comic strip shows Calvin in school. When the teacher asks if there are any questions, Calvin raises his hand and says, "What is the point of human existence?"

The teacher says, "I meant any questions about the subject at hand," to which Calvin replies, "Frankly, I'd like to have the issue resolved before expending any more energy on this."[14]

As usual, Calvin was right on. If we don't have the answer to the purpose question, then what's the point of anything else? The Bible reveals God's purpose in creating us—a purpose we discover when we come to know Him. Walking with a sense of His purpose gives meaning and significance to everything we do.

May He grant you according to your heart's desire,
And fulfill all your purpose.
PSALM 20:4

Life Choices

I heard of a college professor who reminded his students before every test: "You can take this class one of two ways: take it seriously or take it over!"

It would be nice if life offered us that same option. Who wouldn't like a second or third chance to get things right? But the Bible says we only live life once, and after that comes the judgment. Since there is no "do over" in life, we should take it seriously the first time. Fortunately, God has given us a Book with the answers to all of life's tests. With His help, we can lead a life of abundance, and even our mistakes can be made into something good.

Choosing to live in harmony with God and His Word is the best way to approach life.

I have taught you in the way of wisdom;
I have led you in right paths.
When you walk, your steps will not be hindered,
And when you run, you will not stumble.
PROVERBS 4:11–12

Conversion

Years ago, an employee at the Ford Motor Company in Detroit became a Christian and was baptized. The first thing he did was return a number of tools he had stolen from the company. When his boss asked Henry Ford what should be done, he said, "Dam up the Detroit River and baptize the entire city!"

That's the way conversion to Christ is supposed to work—changes should be evident to those who know us. The Bible says when we believe in Christ, our old life is put away and a new life is begun—it's like being "born again."

Conversion requires an action on our part—believe.

 So they said, "Believe on the Lord Jesus Christ, and you will be saved, you and your household."
ACTS 16:31

Opinions

Did you know that anytime a football game is broadcast on television, there are more quarterbacks than players of any other position? There is one on the field, four or five more on the sidelines, thousands in the stands, and millions more in living rooms all across America.

One of the privileges of living in a free country is that everyone can express his or her opinion—on football or anything else. But the value of an opinion is based on the authority of the one giving it. And the Bible says that in the final analysis, only God's opinions will stand.

Take the time to discover what God thinks. No one's opinion matters more.

The works of his hands are faithful and just;
all his precepts are trustworthy.
They are steadfast for ever and ever,
done in faithfulness and uprightness.
PSALM 111:7-8 NIV

Second Coming

A family was discussing the Second Coming of Christ after church one Sunday. The father concluded the discussion by encouraging each of his children to live every day as if it were their last. His teenage son replied, "I tried that once and you grounded me for a month!"

If you knew today was your last day on earth, how would you spend it? The Bible says Christ will return without warning—at a time we least expect. In fact, He could return today! If you're not sure how to prepare for that event, the Bible can tell you how.

Accept the Christ of Scripture, and be attentive to how you live, knowing that your actions will have eternal consequences.

Whoever confesses that Jesus is the Son of God, God abides in him, and he in God.

1 JOHN 4:15 NIV

Peer Pressure

An elderly lady was celebrating her 102nd birthday at a gathering of friends and family. When she was asked what she most enjoyed about being 102 years old, she replied, "The lack of peer pressure!"

Since most of us aren't her age, we probably still have to deal with peer pressure at times. We're all tempted to change our behavior based on how we think others will respond. But the Bible encourages us to make God's opinion the most important. He's the one whose response to our decisions matters most.

When you seek to please God above all others, He sees your heart and is pleased. And it becomes much easier to resist others' opinions when we are confident of God's approval.

On the contrary, we speak as men approved by God to be entrusted with the gospel. We are not trying to please men but God, who tests our hearts.

1 THESSALONIANS 2:4 NIV

God

One day a distraught young university student burst into a pastor's study and announced he could no longer believe in God. Once he described the God he no longer believed in, the pastor responded, "Well, we're in the same boat then. I don't believe in that God either."

Many people who reject God are rejecting a straw man, a figment of their own imagination. Fortunately, the Bible tells us plainly who God is and what He is like. Anyone interested in not believing in God should check their image of Him against the image presented in the Bible before making a final decision.

When we come to the Bible with an open heart and with a prayer for understanding, we get a glimpse of who God really is. We discover His goodness, His justice, His kindness, and His amazing love. This is a God well worth knowing and serving.

 God did this so that men would seek him and perhaps reach out for him and find him, though he is not far from each one of us.
ACTS 17:27 NIV

Money

Forbes magazine tracks the status of the world's wealthiest people. They also have reported on the connection between money and happiness. *Forbes* says that surveys have found the same level of happiness among the four hundred richest people in the world as they found in the Maasai herdsmen of East Africa.[15]

Most people who read those surveys and who aren't rich believe they would be the exception—that wealth would make them incredibly happy. The Bible says that people with eternal natures can't be made truly happy by temporal things. Money is useful and necessary—but it can never buy the happiness we seek.

Look for God's purpose for money, and you will discover what's most important is seeking Him. When God is first in your life, He'll always meet your material needs, but more importantly, He will make your soul prosper.

The LORD will guide you continually, And satisfy your soul in drought, And strengthen your bones;
You shall be like a watered garden, And like a spring of water, whose waters do not fail. ISAIAH 58:11

Hope

A Little League baseball player was in right field when his dad arrived late to the game and called to him from the sideline to see how it was going. "It's seventeen to nothing right now," the little guy yelled to his dad. "But as soon as we get to bat, things'll get better."

Ah, the optimism of youth. Maybe that's why Jesus said adults need to be more like children—hopeful and unencumbered by pessimism and negativism. Could you use a little hope right now? The Bible is full of hope for those who will take time to discover it.

Let God fill you with childlike hope and joy today. No matter what you're facing, good days are ahead.

Therefore whoever humbles himself as this little child is the greatest in the kingdom of heaven.
MATTHEW 18:4

Expectation

In Union Grove, Wisconsin, mentally disabled children receive Christian love and nurture at a place called Shepherd's Home. But they have a problem at Shepherd's Home with keeping the windows clean. Every day the children press their faces against the glass, wondering if that will be the day Jesus returns.

Expectation can get us out of bed in the morning and keep us going during the day. However, many people are not expecting Jesus Christ to return. The Bible says He could return at any time to gather together those who are expecting Him—a good reason to live with dirty windows.

Don't be surprised if living in expectation of Christ's return changes your life completely. I can't think of a better way to approach each day.

For we were saved in this hope, but hope that is seen is not hope; for why does one still hope for what he sees? But if we hope for what we do not see, we eagerly wait for it with perseverance.

ROMANS 8:24-25

Speech

While the young farming couple was in the kitchen fixing dinner, the visiting minister asked their little boy what they were having. "Goat," the boy replied. "Are you sure?" the minister asked. "Yep. I heard Paw say, 'We might as well have the old goat for dinner and get it over with.'"

Ouch! Rule number one: never say something about someone else behind his back that you wouldn't be willing to say to him in person. The Bible puts it this way: let all your speech be edifying—let your speech be words which build people up, not tear them down.

Following God's guidelines for edifying speech can be a challenge—what you say is deeply connected to who you are. That's why it's best to watch your tongue while also asking God to change your heart.

 Let no corrupt word proceed out of your mouth, but what is good for necessary edification, that it may impart grace to the hearers.
EPHESIANS 4:29

Signs from God

The comedian and actor Woody Allen said he wished he could receive some kind of sign from God—like a large deposit made in his name in a Swiss bank. A lot of people would probably appreciate that kind of sign!

The Bible records how a group of religious leaders asked Jesus Christ for a sign to prove that He was the Son of God. He told them there was only one sign left that they should watch for: His resurrection from the dead. That sign would give them—and anyone else—the proof they needed if they really wanted to believe.

We all see signs of God's power in our own lives. But nothing could be more important to our faith than Christ's resurrection. The next time you find yourself wishing for a sign, take time to remember what God has already done.

Praise be to the God and Father of our Lord Jesus Christ! In his great mercy he has given us new birth into a living hope through the resurrection of Jesus Christ from the dead.

1 PETER 1:3 NIV

Slow to Speak

Here's a little piece of verse that carries a wise message:

> If your lips you would keep from slips,
> Five things observe with care:
> Of whom you speak, to whom you speak,
> And how and when and where.

I don't know who wrote this rhyme, but he or she may have been reading a verse in the Bible that says, "Be. . .slow to speak" (James 1:19). All of us have had the experience of saying something and immediately wishing we hadn't. But words, once spoken, are gone forever. And if they were hurtful or unwise words, our regret is all the more real.

Heeding the Bible's advice to choose our words carefully will keep us from feeling that sting of regret. Better yet, it will nurture our efforts to speak helpfully and lovingly into the lives of others.

 Let your speech always be with grace, seasoned with salt, that you may know how you ought to answer each one.
COLOSSIANS 4:6

Understanding

Henny Youngman, king of the one-liners, used to say that his mother-in-law was so concerned with neatness that she spread out a newspaper under the cuckoo clock—just in case.

All of us know people who are a challenge to live with, and we are sometimes a challenge ourselves. So what do we do in those situations? Perhaps something the Bible suggests would help. It says we ought to extend the same understanding and forgiveness to others that God extends to us. After all, if He can extend grace to us, we ought to be able to extend that same grace to others.

When we think about God's unconditional love in our own lives, we suddenly find it much, much easier to overlook the quirks and flaws of others.

Therefore, whatever you want men to do to you, do also to them, for this is the Law and the Prophets.
MATTHEW 7:12

The Glory of Man

The humanistic French philosopher Voltaire wrote that animals have three advantages over men: they don't have theologians who tell them what to do, their funerals cost them nothing, and no one starts a lawsuit over their estate. On those three points the cranky old philosopher may be right.

But what about art and music and sports and literature and love and marriage and discovery and achievement! Man has it all over the animals in the really important things because we're created in the image of God. Yes, life is complicated at times. But most of the time, it's a glorious adventure.

God has a wonderful plan for mankind: He created us to reflect His glory. He's given us a central role to play in His story of creation.

Slow down a second and thank Him today for the wonder of your life.

 For You have made him a little lower than the angels,
And You have crowned him with glory and honor.
PSALM 8:5

Accomplishment

I have heard the woodpecker set forth as a model for mankind: the woodpecker uses his head and just pecks away until he finishes his job. Sounds like good advice to me. Sometimes in the spiritual life we forget that God has given us strong minds and strong backs. We can figure things out and often achieve them by creativity and hard work.

The Bible says we are created in God's image, which means in part that we love to accomplish great things. We can't create worlds, of course, but we can create things that make a world of difference in peoples' lives.

God wants you to have a sense of accomplishment. What task, goal, or dream do you think He might be calling you to today? Whatever you do, do it to the best of your abilities in order to bring glory to God.

 For we are His workmanship, created in Christ Jesus for good works, which God prepared beforehand that we should walk in them.

EPHESIANS 2:10

1 minute a day

Courage

The American poet John Greenleaf Whittier wrote these arresting words: "For of all said words of tongue or pen, The saddest are these: 'It might have been.'"[16]

Another writer, Tim McMahon, wrote, "Risk-taking is inherently failure-prone. Otherwise it would be called sure-thing-taking."

Don't put off reaching for your dreams because of a fear of failure. God will use failure to cultivate courage and determination. Failures are nothing more than rungs on the ladder to success. If you'll just keep pursuing, you'll soon find yourself at the top of that ladder.

If you have a dream, but also have fears, it only means you're human. Ask God for courage to climb the ladder to your dreams today. He will help you keep moving in the right direction.

Be strong and of good courage, do not fear nor be afraid of them; for the LORD your God, He is the One who goes with you. He will not leave you nor forsake you.

DEUTERONOMY 31:6

Communication

A magazine cartoon once showed a professor beginning a lecture on the practice of communication. He said, "Communication is any modus operandi by or through which eventuates the reciprocal transposition of information between or among entities or groups via commonly understood systems of symbols, signs, or behavioral patterns of activity."

Did you get that? I am so glad God communicates with us in ways that are simple to understand. For instance, He says to us, "I love you unconditionally," and "Love your neighbor," and "Trust in Me." When we think about what God asks us to do, we realize that it's pretty simple, really.

God wants you to know Him and His Word. Read His Word with an open heart and open mind. When you do, you will hear from Him clearly and distinctly.

Then you will call upon Me and go and pray to Me, and I will listen to you. And you will seek Me and find Me, when you search for Me with all your heart.
JEREMIAH 29:12–13

Heavenly Treasures

As she approached her ninetieth birthday, a woman thought about the new batch of small knickknacks and porcelain art objects her friends and family usually gave her as presents. When her children were planning her birthday celebration she said, "This year, all I want are hugs and kisses—two things I won't have to dust!"

Whoever said, "You can't take it with you" was right. And the Bible says that instead of storing up treasures on earth, we ought to store them up in heaven where we can enjoy them for eternity. No dusting, no garage sales—just the pleasure of God's gifts.

The rewards you receive for serving God will be worth far more than earthly achievements—they'll last forever, and you won't have to worry about keeping them safe from burglars and thieves. Get involved with God today and discover His many blessings.

 Lay up for yourselves treasures in heaven, where neither moth nor rust destroys and where thieves do not break in and steal. For where your treasure is, there your heart will be also.

MATTHEW 6:20–21

Not of the World

I read about a man who knew he was out of step with the world when a thief broke into his car and stole his CD player but left all his CDs behind. Anybody who tries to stay in step with the world these days will find himself exhausted, confused, or broke—or all of the above!

The Bible talks about being in the world but not of the world. After all, it says, this world is only temporary—it's nothing that will last. We should devote our attention to pleasing God, not chasing after the things of this world. His gifts are eternal, but trends and tastes change with the tides.

Far better to live in step with God and be up-to-date forever.

 But you are a chosen people, a royal priesthood, a holy nation, a people belonging to God, that you may declare the praises of him who called you out of darkness into his wonderful light.
1 PETER 2:9 NIV

Redeem the Time

We often hear people say as they get older, "I'm just as productive now as when I was young." I heard one wag say that anybody who is doing as much at age sixty as he did at age twenty wasn't doing all that much at age twenty to begin with!

Whatever our age, the best way to live is with the pedal to the metal. When the Bible talks about living that way, it talks about redeeming the time—buying up every opportunity to live productively. A minute, day, month, or year wasted is time we will never see again.

Time is precious, so don't waste a minute of your life. Carpe diem—seize the day. There are so many wonderful things with which to fill our days, if we're only willing to get moving.

 "Walk in wisdom toward those who are outside, redeeming the time."
COLOSSIANS 4:5

God's Omnipotence

Go into the laboratories of mankind's great universities and research facilities and you'll be impressed with what has been done. But sit in a meadow under a tree watching cows graze, and you'll quickly see man's limits: no scientist has yet figured out how to turn grass into milk.

Man is brilliant, creative, and industrious, to be sure. But there are limits to what we can do. For some things man is adequate—for everything else there is God. The Bible says that nothing—absolutely nothing—is impossible for Him.

If you have reached the limits of your problem-solving ability, turn to God. His strength and resources are unlimited, as is His love for you. Let Him take the reins in your life—that's one thing you can do, and it's the one thing that you will never, ever regret.

The things which are impossible with men are possible with God.
LUKE 18:27

Truth

I read once where the truth about any man is probably found somewhere between the opinion of his mother and the opinion of his mother-in-law. That theory can be applied in many realms of life—the truth is usually in the middle of two extremes.

One place where we don't have to find the middle in order to find the truth is in the Bible. In fact, the Bible says it's not a collection of men's opinions or interpretations. Rather, it's the truth of God.

What questions do you have about life? Do you want to know who you really are? Are you curious about the future or the state of the world around you? Do you want to know how to please God?

If you want to find out the truth about yourself—or anything else—start first with the Bible. There you'll find the unbending, unrelenting truth.

 Sanctify them by Your truth. Your word is truth.
JOHN 17:17

Appreciation

One day, a teacher asked her students, "Which is more important—the sun or the moon?" One eager student quickly replied, "The moon. Because the moon gives us light at night when it's dark. The sun just gives us light in the day when we don't really need it."

When I read that story, it made me wonder how often I take for granted those who make my life easier. The Bible says no one should be taken for granted—that every person is important. If there's someone in your life who needs appreciating, why not communicate your appreciation to that person today? I guarantee you'll make their day, and your words of gratitude will help them keep doing the good work they're doing.

God wants to use you to encourage those around you. Be a willing vessel in that effort today.

Therefore comfort each other and edify one another, just as you also are doing. And we urge you, brethren, to recognize those who labor among you, and are over you in the Lord and admonish you.
1 THESSALONIANS 5:11–12

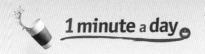
Sowing and Reaping

Listen carefully to this saying: "Lucky parents who have fine children usually have lucky children who have fine parents." In other words, parents who think their kids are great usually have kids who think their parents are great. Said another way, what goes around comes around.

The Bible puts it this way: we reap what we sow. If you're a nice friend, you'll probably have lots of nice friends. If you're generous, people will probably be generous toward you.

We get out of life what we put into it. It's amazing how that principle lets us create the very world we've dreamed of living in simply by paying attention to our actions. Make sure what you're putting in is what you want to receive.

But the path of the just is like the shining sun,
That shines ever brighter unto the perfect day.
PROVERBS 4:18

Perfectionism

A young man vowed not to get married until he found the perfect woman. At last he found her, but discovered she had vowed not to marry until she found the perfect man. At last report, neither of them was married.

Perfectionism can drain the fun right out of a great life. We can ruin our own lives, or the lives of others, by embracing the belief that human perfection is possible in this world. It isn't. The greatest proof of that is the fact that God sent His perfect Son into the world to save us from our human imperfections.

None of us will attain perfection in this life; but by God's grace, we can keep striving for holiness. We can also accept His forgiveness for our shortcomings—and share His unconditional love with those around us.

 And above all things have fervent love for one another, for "love will cover a multitude of sins."
1 PETER 4:8

God's Calling

After spending a considerable amount of money over many years to send their son to the finest piano teachers, the boy's parents were always eager for him to play for guests. One evening, after the boy played a couple of fairly simple pieces, his father said, "Okay, son, now play something expensive."

While the father's choice of words is debatable, he made a good point: we ought to live up to the potential we have been given. The Bible says it this way: walk worthy of your calling. When we fail to live up to our potential, we waste what God has invested in us.

God has a calling on each of our lives. With His help, we can live up to that calling—but we must diligently strive to be the best we can.

I, therefore, the prisoner of the Lord, beseech you to walk worthy of the calling with which you were called, with all lowliness and gentleness, with longsuffering, bearing with one another in love.
EPHESIANS 4:1-2

Abundant Giving

One Friday afternoon a teenager was leaving for a weekend church retreat at the beach. He asked his dad, "Do you think I could have a little spending money to take with me?" "Sure," the father replied. "How little do you think you'll need?"

What if we asked God a similar question: "God, do you think you could give us a little help in living?" "Sure," God could reply. "How little help do you think you'll need?" But the Bible says God does just the opposite. He gave us His Son and continually gives us more than we even think to ask for. He provides abundantly, extravagantly for His children, giving us more grace than we could ever need.

As we deal with the people in our lives—our children, our friends, and coworkers—we would do well to follow His example, seeking to bless others extravagantly.

 Oh, how great is Your goodness,
Which You have laid up for those who fear You,
Which You have prepared for those who trust in You.
PSALM 31:19

Resistance

When one of my children attended college in western North Carolina, I used to love driving through the mountains when we'd visit. I noticed what I've seen in other mountainous regions—the roads always seem to follow the streams. Water always finds the path of least resistance.

I've also noticed in life how the path of least resistance can lead from the heights to the depths. If we want to go higher, we have to endure the strain of climbing uphill.

The Bible says climbing uphill makes us stronger, even though it's harder. The rewards of taking the more difficult path are great. The next time you're choosing a path, choose the best one, not the easiest one. You'll be better for it.

 Enter by the narrow gate; for wide is the gate and broad is the way that leads to destruction, and there are many who go in by it.

MATTHEW 7:13

Gratitude

A man from mountainous Colorado moved to Texas and built a house with a big picture window. But he complained there was nothing to see except flat prairies. A man from Texas moved to Colorado and built a house with a big picture window, and he complained he couldn't see anything because the mountains were in the way.

As the late comedienne Gilda Radner used to say, "It's always something!"[17] One of the Bible's secrets to happiness is learning to be grateful for what we have—and we have a lot. God gives us many, many gifts, from health and salvation to the comfort of relationships to the pleasure of living.

If you've been tempted to complain about things recently, try a little gratitude instead. You might be surprised how it changes your perspective.

As you therefore have received Christ Jesus the Lord, so walk in Him, rooted and built up in Him and established in the faith, as you have been taught, abounding in it with thanksgiving.
COLOSSIANS 2:6–7

Starting Over

A man went to a nursery to select some trees for his yard. While there, he noticed a sign that said, "The best time to plant a tree was fifteen years ago. The second best time is today."

Too often we despair over the things we realize we should have done years ago: get more education, save more for retirement, or spend more time with our children. The discouragement causes us to say to ourselves, "What's the use? I blew my chance." But the Bible's perspective on missed opportunities is that God can make up for the years that we let slip away. It's never too late for Him to do a new work in our lives.

If you feel like you've blown it, talk to God. He can redeem even the worst tragedies and the biggest mistakes.

Behold, I will do a new thing,
Now it shall spring forth;
Shall you not know it?
I will even make a road in the wilderness
And rivers in the desert.
ISAIAH 43:19

God's Voice

At the South Pole, after mother penguins have hatched their young, they return to the sea to feed, leaving the babies in the care of their fathers. When they return weeks later, the mothers search through the crowd of thousands of penguins until mother and child recognize each others' voices and are reunited.

The Bible says Jesus and His followers are like that—we must learn to recognize His voice amidst all the confusing spiritual voices in our world today. If we aren't careful, we could be led down the wrong path spiritually because we don't recognize Jesus' voice through His Word.

Spend time with your Shepherd so that you'll know His voice. He'll lead you in the right path if you'll just follow Him.

My sheep hear My voice, and I know them, and they follow Me. And I give them eternal life, and they shall never perish; neither shall anyone snatch them out of My hand.

JOHN 10:27–28

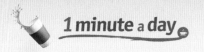

Love for God

There's a pretty good possibility that you have used the word *love* today. You may have told your spouse or your children that you love them, or you may have told a coworker how much you love your new computer.

We freely use the word "love" in our daily conversation—except for one place: we don't tell God that we love Him as often as we should. No one has done more for us than He has, yet somehow we feel strange saying, "I love You, Lord."

We need to practice telling the Lord we love Him. He loves us and wants to hear of our love for Him. The more often you tell Him, the more natural it will feel. And as your love for Him deepens, you'll be more inclined to live a life that worships and adores Him.

 Thanks be to God for His indescribable gift!
2 CORINTHIANS 9:15

God's Work

Even those of us who are not experts on art have learned to pick out the works of many artists. For instance, I can usually tell when I'm looking at a painting by Picasso, Salvador Dali, Vincent van Gogh, Rembrandt, or Andrew Wyeth. Even if I'm not sure, when someone tells me who the artist is, I immediately say, "Ah, yes—I recognize it now."

Did you know the works of God have defining characteristics like those of a great artist? God's works are always defined by love, sacrifice, compassion, righteousness, and justice. That means the works of Christians should bear the same marks.

God has asked us to show the world what He is like. Let us live our lives in such a way that people see God's character in us.

"You are the light of the world. A city that is set on a hill cannot be hidden. . . . Let your light so shine before men, that they may see your good works and glorify your Father in heaven."

MATTHEW 5:14, 16

Influence

The dictionary says an influence is a power that affects a person, thing, or course of events—and here's the most important part—*especially a power which operates without any apparent effort.*[18] The idea that I'm continually being influenced by forces I don't even notice or recognize makes me a little nervous.

If that's true, then it also means I can be a quiet influence in this world. Without making a big fuss about it, I can influence people with love, honesty, cheerfulness, respect, patience, kindness, and good deeds—just like Jesus Christ influenced people in His day.

Those small things we do—showing mercy to another person, being diligent, making choices with integrity—can make a big difference in someone else's life. Make sure your day-to-day actions are having a positive influence on others.

 Do everything without complaining or arguing, so that you may become blameless and pure, children of God without fault in a crooked and depraved generation, in which you shine like stars in the universe as you hold out the word of life.
PHILIPPIANS 2:14–16 NIV

Generous Living

Over the years, I have discovered a trait held in common by the happiest and most successful people I have met. And that trait is generosity. Generous people give away their time, their advice, their money, their books—they'll give away almost anything. Generous people have concluded that nothing is more valuable than helping another person succeed.

And I'll tell you something else that generous people seem to possess—they possess faith in and gratitude toward God. The deeper our understanding of God's generosity, the more compelled we are to be as generous as He is. And that means giving whenever we can, looking to the interests of others rather than to our own interests.

What can you give to someone today? That person will be blessed by your generosity—as will you.

Honor the LORD with your possessions,
And with the firstfruits of all your increase;
So your barns will be filled with plenty,
And your vats will overflow with new wine.
PROVERBS 3:9–10

Knowledge of God's Word

I read somewhere that it takes ten years to master a body of knowledge. And that's for someone who studies the subject thoroughly in graduate school and then works and continues to study in the field for several more years full-time as a vocation.

If it takes a professional ten years to master the information in his field, think how long it will take us to gain a working knowledge of God's Word if we only devote five to ten minutes a day to the task. If we're going to really experience the Bible, know it well, let it change us, we have to make our study of Scripture a higher priority.

The more time we make in our lives for mining the riches of the Bible, the better we will know its Author.

Oh, how I love Your law!
It is my meditation all the day. . . .
How sweet are Your words to my taste,
Sweeter than honey to my mouth!

PSALM 119:97, 103

Discipline (Training)

Medical researchers tell us that aggressive mental exercise is one of the best ways to ward off the senility and dementia that sometimes accompany old age. Work puzzles, learn a foreign language, take community college courses—anything that forces the brain to stay active and alert.

We know that physical and mental exercises keep our body and mind in good shape, but did you know spiritual exercises are important, too? Praying, meditating on Bible verses, fasting, serving others—all these are spiritual disciplines that renew our spirit and keep apathy at bay. The more you exercise your spirit, the stronger it gets.

Discover the benefits of spiritual discipline. Nothing will make your spiritual life richer or more satisfying.

Do you not know that those who run in a race all run, but one receives the prize? Run in such a way that you may obtain it.

1 CORINTHIANS 9:24

Gratification

The market for mega-yachts is exploding around the world. These luxury boats, ranging in size from one hundred to five hundred feet long, are being ordered as fast as builders can produce them. What is driving this market? As a high-ranking marketing executive for Island Global Yachting, Sheri Wilson-Gray said, "Such yachts are not at all about transportation. They are about ego gratification."[19]

Does it really take a fifty-million-dollar boat to satisfy the human soul? I'll never know, but I have found a number of things that do gratify me: my family, my friends, fulfilling my calling from God. I especially look forward to His welcoming me home to heaven. I could never buy things as precious as these with any amount of money, but they're of untold value to my soul.

The truth is that when we focus on what really matters, we experience a greater satisfaction than the world could ever offer us.

 Why do you spend money for what is not bread,
And your wages for what does not satisfy?
Listen carefully to Me, and eat what is good,
And let your soul delight itself in abundance.
ISAIAH 55:2

Relationships

"You can't live with them and you can't live without them." That old expression has been applied to lots of things, and it also applies to relationships. Nothing takes more work than keeping relationships healthy—and nothing keeps us more emotionally healthy than good relationships. Sometimes it's a challenge to live with them, but we certainly can't live without them.

The apostle Paul says we ought to love others the way God loves us. It stands to reason that if my relationship with God is good because of how He loves me, my relationships with others will be good if I love them the same way.

When we study the ways in which God relates to people, we discover keys to healthy relationships.

Today, adopt His selflessness and love. In the process, you will be a blessing to others, and you will create healthier, happier relationships with the people you care about.

 No one has seen God at any time. If we love one another, God abides in us, and His love has been perfected in us.
1 JOHN 4:12

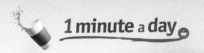

Unfaithfulness

The wounds suffered by the unfaithfulness of a friend are severe. And I'm not just talking about unfaithfulness in marriage. Any breach of loyalty sends the same message: You are not important enough for me to keep my word or fulfill my responsibilities to you.

We often assign value to our lives by assessing how others value us. And sometimes we come up short—sometimes people hurt us with their lack of concern for us. Fortunately, there is One person who values us so highly that He will always be faithful, who will always keep His word, no matter what. The Bible tells us that person is God.

If you've felt the sting of someone's unfaithfulness, turn to God and let Him heal that wound with His faithful love today. What's even better is that as we experience His faithfulness to us, we become more faithful to others.

Where can I go from Your Spirit?
Or where can I flee from Your presence?
If I ascend into heaven, You are there;
If I make my bed in hell, behold, You are there.
PSALM 139:7–8

The Cross

You can tell America is changing when you hear small children ask their parents why so many churches have plus signs on top of them. Or when you notice that the cross has become the most popular piece of jewelry worn by everyone from supermodels to rock stars.

In the Roman Empire, the cross was a sign of death, not a fashion statement. The Bible tells us how Christ was crucified on a cross like a common criminal—but for a very uncommon reason. He died so that we wouldn't have to.

His death was more than just a good deed worth remembering. It was the event that brought us over from death to life. The next time you see a cross on the top of a building or around someone's neck, remember what it stands for and say a prayer of thanks.

He humbled Himself and became obedient to
the point of death, even the death of the cross.
PHILIPPIANS 2:8

Education

I have read that a project manager at a large corporation once made a mistake that cost the company 10 million dollars. He immediately volunteered to resign. The company's response was amazing: "Resign?" they said. "We just spent ten million dollars on your education! We're not about to let you go now."

The company's response to an employee's failure is similar to how God looks at our failures in life—as opportunities to grow and become wiser. The Bible says God walks with us through difficult times so we won't quit. He has invested something far more valuable than money in us, and He's not about to give up on His investment.

Let God teach you and train you in the ways of wisdom. You'll never find a wiser or more caring Teacher.

 O God, You have taught me from my youth;
And to this day I declare Your wondrous works.
PSALM 71:17

Jesus

The teacher of an American history class gave his students an assignment during class: compile a list of the eleven greatest Americans. A few minutes later, he asked one young man if he had finished the assignment. "Almost," the boy said. "I just can't decide on a quarterback."

If you had to identify the greatest person who has ever lived, who would you choose? Many people, including lots of non-Christians, would choose Jesus Christ. The combination of His selfless lifestyle and personal sacrifice, not to mention the good that has been accomplished in His name, sets Him apart from all others.

Unlike other historical figures, of course, Jesus is still available to talk to and share life with today. We can encounter Him in the Bible as well as through prayer. Experience Him in a fresh way today.

 And when the Sabbath had come, He began to teach in the synagogue. And many hearing Him were astonished, saying, "Where did this Man get these things? And what wisdom is this which is given to Him, that such mighty works are performed by His hands!" MARK 6:2

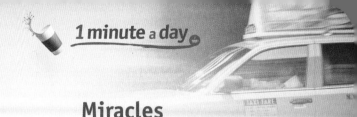

Miracles

Two men were duck hunting, and one started bragging about what a good shot he was. A duck flew by and the bragger fired—and the duck flew on without a scratch. After a moment, the bragger said, "My friend, you are witnessing a miracle. There flies a dead duck!"

I don't know about you, but I'm thinking that really wasn't a miracle. But I know what is: the Bible says every human being is dead in their sins until Christ makes them alive with new life. That's the miracle of the new birth—to be dead one moment and made alive the next.

History, Scripture, and our own lives testify that God's restorative power is great—He can even create life out of death! Take comfort in His miraculous power today, knowing that He's given you an awesome gift.

For the wages of sin is death, but the gift of God is eternal life in Christ Jesus our Lord.
ROMANS 6:23

The Devil

The British scholar and writer C. S. Lewis wrote that we generally make one of two errors when considering the devil. Either we give him more attention than he deserves, or we ignore him completely.[20] So where do we find the balance—the truth about the devil?

Not in popular culture. If we think of him with his proverbial red suit, pointy tail, and pitchfork, we make a laughing matter out of something serious. We need an authoritative source for learning about the devil, and that would be the Bible—the only book that chronicles his past, present, and future.

Prayerfully open your Bible for a look at the devil and let God show you how to be wary of his schemes—as well as how God has overwhelmingly defeated him.

> Be sober, be vigilant; because your adversary the devil walks about like a roaring lion, seeking whom he may devour.
> 1 PETER 5:8

Religion

Travel to the four corners of the globe, and you will find religion of some kind in every region of the earth. Since the dawn of time, man has been trying to find the God who created and rules the universe. Man's attempt to find God is best defined by the word *religion.* God's effort to find lost humanity, however, is what the New Testament calls *Christianity.*

Is this just playing with words, or is there a difference between Christianity and religion? There is a difference. The Bible says that God has taken the initiative to reach out to the world—to offer mankind a free gift of eternal life. That's Christianity. Religion attempts to know and please God through human effort.

Thank God today for reaching out to us through His Son Jesus, and for the freedom to come to Him just as we are.

 For God did not send His Son into the world to condemn the world, but that the world through Him might be saved.
JOHN 3:17

Self-Protection

Very few places in the world today have walled cities;
but in ancient times, they were commonplace. Walls were
a necessary means of protection, and they required regular
maintenance and strengthening lest an enemy exploit their
disrepair. Not to have a strong wall was to put one's life at risk.

Interestingly, an ancient proverb in the Bible says
that a city with a broken-down wall is like a man without
self-control. That's a powerful image! Without self-control, I
make myself vulnerable to all sorts of invading impulses and
destructive temptations. Fortunately, God offers to make His
spiritual walls available to all who desire them.

Let God's Spirit cultivate in you self-control, and you will
see your life flourish and prosper.

His divine power has given to us all things that
pertain to life and godliness, through the knowledge
of Him who called us by glory and virtue.
2 PETER 1:3

Cheating

The last several years have seen headlines detailing cheating at all levels of society: at colleges and universities, huge corporations, athletic departments, even at our nation's military academies, where the honor code is a sacred trust. In his book author David Callahan describes a new "cheating culture"[21] that seems to justify cheating if needed.

But is cheating ever acceptable? Who would want to get credit for something they never actually accomplished? Apparently a lot of people. But a day is coming, the Bible says, when everything done in secret will be brought to light. Better to be honest now than to have cheating made public in the future.

Holding to a high personal standard frees us from fear of detection. True achievement brings real satisfaction.

 Keep sound wisdom and discretion; So they will be life to your soul And grace to your neck. Then you will walk safely in your way, And your foot will not stumble.
PROVERBS 3:21–23

Disappointment

I have finally discovered the way to avoid 99 percent of all disappointments in life: go home, draw the blinds, lock the door, and take the phone off the hook. In other words, drop out of life altogether. The problem is, this solution itself would end up being a terribly disappointing way to live.

The hard truth is that disappointment is inevitable in this life. Even if others don't disappoint you, you'll surely disappoint yourself.

Discouragement, however, is not inevitable. You can learn to handle disappointment by reading the Bible's realistic descriptions of the disappointments of life—as well as God's continual work in our lives—and how to handle setbacks without giving up.

One thing in life is sure: God will never disappoint. Put your hope in Him. No disappointment can steal your joy.

Because God wanted to make the unchanging nature of his purpose very clear to the heirs of what was promised, he confirmed it with an oath. God did this so that . . . we who have fled to take hold of the hope offered to us may be greatly encouraged. We have this hope as an anchor for the soul, firm and secure. HEBREWS 6:17–19 NIV

1 minute a day

Singleness

If you are a single person, you probably know about the hottest business trend on the Internet. In fact, you may have helped this sector along. Singles looking for meaningful relationships is currently a growth industry, and Web sites that facilitate that process are exploding.

It's hard to argue with the concept—marriage is a wonderful experience. But so is being single! There is no better time to establish life goals, sort out priorities, and get to know and enjoy other people than as a single person. The Bible also suggests that singles enjoy a special privilege: undivided fellowship with the living God.

Whatever your station in life, thank God. He gives us the blessing of marriage, as well as a unique experience of His companionship during our single years. He has a rich life planned for you, if you'll simply accept His gifts today and trust Him for the future.

 The LORD shall preserve your going out and your coming in. From this time forth, and even forevermore.
PSALM 121:8

Friendships

First there was *Cheers,* the show about a place "where everybody knows your name." Then came *Seinfeld,* a show about four zany friends. And then there was actually a show called *Friends.* These shows, and others like them, are immensely popular because they focus on something we all want: friendships.

Modern cultures have been described as full of "intimate strangers"—people who are physically close but emotionally distant. The Bible counters that image with a picture of communities of people sharing life together as close friends—physically, emotionally, and spiritually. Their friendship with each other is modeled on God's friendship with them.

That community is available to us as we nurture our friendship with God and with others. One of God's richest blessings to us is the gift of friendship.

 We, being many, are one body in Christ, and individually members of one another.
ROMANS 12:5

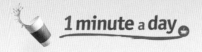

1 minute a day

Self-Acceptance

Psychologists tell us that self-acceptance is a big problem in our culture. Probably in childhood, we learn that someone doesn't like something about us. And we subconsciously agree. They're right, we think. I don't like that part of me, either.

Then, as adults, we search for a mentor, or authority figure, to tell us we're okay. I'm not an authority figure, but I do have good news for you: God knows everything about you and says to you today, "I like you—in fact, I love you." In the pages of the Bible, we discover that God is completely accepting of us—no strings attached!

This is powerful news. God's acceptance of us gives us a sense of worth and value, which makes life sweeter and more exciting.

Seek God in prayer and listen for His words of unconditional love.

The LORD has appeared of old to me, saying:
"Yes, I have loved you with an everlasting love;
Therefore with lovingkindness I have drawn you."
JEREMIAH 31:3

Wisdom

How many truly wise people do you know? Not smart people—but wise. To answer that question, let's define wisdom by thinking of it in terms of skill. A wise person is one who is skilled at living life successfully, avoiding the multitudes of entanglements that derail so many along the way.

In light of that definition, do you know many wise people? Are you a wise person? Likely, you want to be. I don't know anyone who sets out to fail morally or otherwise. But we definitely need help in gaining the skill of living. Fortunately, an entire book of the Bible is devoted to that subject.

Spend a little time with the book of Proverbs to discover God's principles for truly successful living. Most importantly, be sure you ask God for wisdom. The Bible says He gives it freely to those who ask Him for it. He wants you to live a good life, and He's just waiting to show you how.

Blessed is every one who fears the LORD,
Who walks in His ways.
When you eat the labor of your hands,
You shall be happy, and it shall be well with you.
PSALM 128:1-2

Wholeness

Philosophers tell us that the idea of something in our minds is a clue that it could exist—like human perfection, for instance. We know we are imperfect beings, and we can imagine what wholeness would be like. Just the thought of wholeness gives us hope that we might someday achieve it.

But man has been striving for wholeness for ages, yet it remains beyond our grasp. We have the desire to be whole—why not the ability? The Bible answers that question and shows us One who was perfection personified. In Scripture we discover His plan to bring us wholeness.

Jesus explained perfection as loving the unlovely. Today, love Jesus' way and be whole!

 Therefore you shall be perfect, just as your Father in heaven is perfect.
MATTHEW 5:48

Grief

The pain of loss can make even the strongest soul weep great tears of grief. Perhaps it is the loss of thousands of fellow citizens in a terrorist attack. Or the loss of a single, cherished friend the day death comes calling. Maybe it's the loss of a dream, a plan, or a purpose.

Whatever the cause, loss is painful. And it is completely normal and understandable. And that pain deserves comfort. The Bible tells us that God is familiar with loss and therefore able to comfort us in our heartbreaks and griefs. If you need a shoulder to weep on, God's are broad and His arms are open.

Discover God's comfort in the pages of Scripture, and bring your broken heart to Him. You'll never find a greater comforter.

 Blessed be the God and Father of our Lord Jesus Christ, the Father of mercies and God of all comfort, who comforts us in all our tribulation, that we may be able to comfort those who are in any trouble, with the comfort with which we ourselves are comforted by God.
2 CORINTHIANS 1:3–4

Service

There aren't many people on Internet job sites trying to get hired as servants or slaves. Nor are there many companies advertising to fill those positions. Servanthood seems to be an outdated concept these days.

But there's one place servanthood is as fresh and timely as ever, and that's in the pages of the Bible. There you'll find numerous examples of people who voluntarily became slaves of Jesus Christ and called themselves that publicly. Once you become a slave of Jesus, becoming a servant to others is a privilege, not a burden. Joyful servanthood is all about who your master is.

When we serve others, we're really serving God—the most worthy Master ever known.

> "Whoever wants to become great among you must be your servant, and whoever wants to be first must be your slave—just as the Son of Man did not come to be served, but to serve, and to give his life as a ransom for many."
>
> MATTHEW 20:26-28 NIV

Church

Many Christians carry around in their minds an unfortunate division between the Church with a capital *C* and the church with a lower case *c*. They know they are members of the universal Church—the body of all believers in Christ—but they don't see a need to join a local church.

The local church is the manifestation of Christ's spiritual body. Not to be an active part of a fellowship of Christians is like joining the Army but never reporting for duty. The book of Acts in the New Testament presents a picture of how exciting life in a local church can be.

Check it out and re-enlist! Then hold on!

And let us consider one another in order to stir up love and good works, not forsaking the assembling of ourselves together, as is the manner of some, but exhorting one another, and so much the more as you see the Day approaching.

HEBREWS 10:24–25

1 minute a day

Personal Peace

Analysts tell us that at any given moment there are numerous wars taking place somewhere in the world. Twenty-four hours a day, 365 days a year, people are fighting with each other. Those statistics are sad, but here's something worse: there are billions of other wars taking place that we rarely hear about.

The heart of every human is a battlefield where fear attacks faith, and flesh wars with spirit; despair attacks hope, and hate battles against love. Fortunately for us, the Bible says that all those personal battles can be won by the Prince of Peace who stands knocking at the door of our heart.

Restful hearts are free to face life's battles confidently and fearlessly.

 And the peace of God, which surpasses all understanding, will guard your hearts and minds through Christ Jesus.
PHILIPPIANS 4:7

Compassion

Compassion is a word that is used a lot but understood little. Many think it means to feel sorry for someone. Actually, *compassion* comes from Latin words that mean "to suffer with." When we have compassion on someone, we suffer with him. Said another way, we feel that person's pain.

To have compassion means we so identify with another person's plight that it affects us the way it affects him. We weep because our friend weeps. The Bible says that Jesus Christ can have compassion on us because He came to earth and identified with us. No one knows our pain better than Jesus.

Christ acted out His compassion. Show yours through your actions.

 And when Jesus went out He saw a great multitude; and He was moved with compassion for them, and healed their sick.

MATTHEW 14:14

Success

I see books today on how to succeed at everything: from love to lifestyles, from money to marriage. Books are valuable, and I read all the good ones I can find. But I measure the principles for success in every book I read by the principles in God's book, the Bible.

I don't know anyone more successful than God. Who else has created a universe and kept it running for eons of time? He also created us—and gave us principles for our own success. Here's a principle God gave to a successful man named Joshua: meditate on Scripture, and follow it carefully.

The result will amaze you! You will experience real and lasting success.

> Do not let this Book of the Law depart from your mouth; meditate on it day and night, so that you may be careful to do everything written in it. Then you will be prosperous and successful.
>
> JOSHUA 1:8 NIV

Trust

The phrase "In God We Trust" first appeared on our coins in 1864 as a result of religious sentiment arising out of the Civil War—and our coins bear that phrase today. But what does it mean to trust in God? We have found it is easier to trust in a sentiment about God than in God himself.

In the Bible, God invites us to place our trust directly in Him for everything. And not just when we don't know the answers. Trust is not something we do just when we need something or are scared. It's what we do because of who God is.

He is a master provider. His faithfulness can never be worn down, and His love for us has no limit. Trust Him.

And those who know Your name will put their trust in You; For You, LORD, have not forsaken those who seek You.
PSALM 9:10

Pride

In just the right amount, pride can be a good thing. An athlete, for instance, can take pride in doing her best whether she wins or not. That kind of confidence and security is healthy. But too much pride can lead to arrogance or self-centeredness. We've all heard that pride goes before a fall, and it's true.

So how do we find the balance? The Bible offers an interesting insight: God gives grace to the humble—grace being divine strength and help. So when we humble ourselves, God helps us to do our best and feel good about who we are.

Doing your best and offering it to God results in great reward.

 And whatever you do, do it heartily, as to the Lord and not to men, knowing that from the Lord you will receive the reward of the inheritance; for you serve the Lord Christ.
COLOSSIANS 3:23-24

Purposeful Living

The next time you cook breakfast, be thankful for the accidental discovery that keeps your eggs from sticking to the pan. A DuPont scientist discovered Teflon accidentally while he was searching for something else. But while experimenting can be a good approach in science, it's usually not very fulfilling in life.

Are you living an experimental life or a purposeful life? Many people today believe they are accidents of evolution and spend their whole lives experimenting to try to figure out the best way to live. But the Bible says you are purposeful and unique, created by a loving God for great and noble reasons. God wants you to live your life on purpose, not accidentally.

Serving your God-given purpose is fulfilling. Pursue that fulfillment today.

 The LORD will fulfill his purpose for me;
your love, O LORD, endures forever—
do not abandon the works of your hands.
PSALM 138:8 NIV

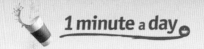
Pain

Whoever first said, "No pain, no gain," was not just a poet, but a wise poet. That little slogan doesn't belong just to the world of athletes or Navy SEALs. It applies to life in general in this way: the deepest lessons of life are usually learned in the midst of the deepest pain.

Pain probes us at levels we've never experienced. And with that probing come deeper insights—about God, and about our lives and ourselves. We learn lessons that make us sharper and stronger for the road ahead, better equipped to live a meaningful, purposeful life.

Let their pain be your gain as you face your personal challenges.

 Weeping may endure for a night,
But joy comes in the morning.
PSALM 30:5

Discouragement

Have you ever taken a close look at the word *discouragement?* At the heart of discouragement is the word *courage.* Therefore, *dis-couragement* is the absence of courage. Anyone who has ever felt discouraged knows that courage is exactly what they lack.

But courage isn't a feeling we have to hope will appear. Courage is nothing more than confidence in God and in the gifts He has given: strength, abilities, purpose, and wisdom, as well as His very presence. The Bible is filled with reasons why the child of God should be en-*couraged*, not dis-*couraged*.

You can keep the blues at bay by building your confidence in God through His Word. He is faithful, good, and loving. Take courage in Who He is!

I would have lost heart, unless I had believed
That I would see the goodness of the LORD
In the land of the living.
Wait on the LORD;
Be of good courage,
And He shall strengthen your heart.
PSALM 27:13–14

Anger

Road rage on the highways has gotten so bad in one state that the legislature passed tougher laws to ticket slow drivers. Apparently slow drivers are to blame for angry outbursts by some enraged motorists. Is that a good idea?—blaming someone else for my anger?

The Bible says something very interesting about anger. It says, "Be angry, and do not sin" (Ephesians 4:26). In other words, check your anger—don't let it cause harm to another person. Granted, there are plenty of temptations to anger in today's world, but the Bible explains how we can learn to keep our cool in a hot situation.

There is no law against self-control.

But the fruit of the Spirit is love, joy, peace, longsuffering, kindness, goodness, faithfulness, gentleness, self-control. Against such there is no law.
GALATIANS 5:22–23

Loneliness

Everyone knows gambling can be addictive. But did you know that teenagers and the elderly are the newest at-risk groups for gambling addiction? Researchers say loneliness is the reason. Whether an elderly person has lost a spouse, or a teenager feels left out, loneliness is real—and it can really hurt.

But did you know it's possible to be alone yet not be lonely? The Bible tells us that Jesus said to His disciples, "I am with you always, even to the end of the age" (Matthew 28:20). No matter how alone we feel, we are promised that God is beside us every day of our lives.

God's promises remind us of God's presence with us at all times.

As the mountains surround Jerusalem,
So the LORD surrounds His people
From this time forth and forever.
PSALM 125:2

Time and Eternity

If you're a fan of jigsaw puzzles, you need to try the aptly-named Eternity puzzle. It consists of 209 pieces, each of which is a compound of thirty-, sixty-, and ninety-degree angles. Introduced in England in June of 1999, the 1-million-pound prize for its completion was awarded over a year later.

While that particular "eternity" may be a difficult puzzle, there is another puzzle called eternity that couldn't be easier to solve: how to be sure of one's eternal life. The Bible's most famous verse, John 3:16, solves the puzzle of eternal life for all who will read it.

Whoever believes in Jesus has eternal life. Puzzle completed!

"Most assuredly, I say to you, he who hears My word and believes in Him who sent Me has everlasting life, and shall not come into judgment, but has passed from death into life."

JOHN 5:24

Temptation

When the American wilderness was being settled, many pioneers and mountain men made their living by setting traps and snares to catch fur-bearing animals. Times have changed, however. Snares of various sorts are rapidly being outlawed in the United States and Europe because of their inhumane impact on wild animals.

But there is one place where snares are still totally legal, and that is the spiritual realm. The Bible says one of the devil's chief strategies is to set tempting snares for his prey—that means you and me. To be forewarned is to be forearmed—if, that is, we heed the warning.

Fortunately, when the snares of temptations do become traps, God is able to free us.

No temptation has overtaken you except such as is common to man; but God is faithful, who will not allow you to be tempted beyond what you are able, but with the temptation will also make the way of escape, that you may be able to bear it.

1 CORINTHIANS 10:13

Endurance

The 1914 expedition of British explorer Ernest Shackleton to Antarctica ended up being legendary, but for all the wrong reasons. The expedition's ship, aptly named *Endurance,* became locked in ice. Twenty-two months later, after one of history's most amazing sagas of survival, Shackleton's crew was rescued.

Most of us can endure more than we think we can. We protest more loudly over the inconvenience of our pain than because we can't endure it. And while most of us will never have to survive months in a frozen landscape, the Bible says endurance results in something indispensable to us all: character.

Character development is more important than personal comfort.

God stands ready to strengthen us if we will only call on Him for help.

 Let us lay aside every weight, and the sin which so easily ensnares us, and let us run with endurance the race that is set before us.
HEBREWS 12:1

Spiritual Deafness

Since forever, wives have accused their husbands of "selective hearing." Now science may be validating that accusation. Researchers in Indiana used MRI scans to prove that men listen primarily with the left side of the brain, while women listen with the left and right.[22]

Whether men listen selectively or not, we'll leave to the researchers. But here's something about hearing we can know for sure: the Bible says we are all spiritually deaf until God does a bit of surgery on our heart.

Mankind hears physically with the ear, but spiritually with the heart. If you'd like to hear God, ask Him to operate on your heart.

Blessed are your eyes for they see,
and your ears for they hear.
MATTHEW 13:16

Converting

There was talk in America years ago about converting our system of weights and measures from the familiar standard system to the metric system. Yards would become meters, miles would become kilometers, and so on. To say the least, it's been a slow conversion.

Some changes take time, but others happen all at once. The Bible says that when a person is born again, he becomes a new creation in a moment of time. He is born again. Yes, the resulting changes in our lifestyle happen gradually, but our conversion—our change from a natural person to a spiritual person—happens at once.

Converting requires an action on our part—believe.

 "Believe on the Lord Jesus Christ, and you will be saved, you and your household."
ACTS 16:31

Impartiality

We often hear on the news that someone in government is calling for an "impartial investigation." Or one person accuses another of not being impartial—of showing favoritism or bias. The very fact that we have to insist on impartiality is sound evidence that we are, by nature, biased people.

Try as we might, it's hard for us to conceal our preferences—and sometimes that can be a problem. Fortunately, the Bible says that God is impartial in all His dealings with us. We never have to worry about whether we have been treated fairly with Him. No one has ever called for an "impartial investigation" of God.

His judgments are right, just and purposeful. He is completely worthy of our trust.

He is the Rock, His work is perfect;
For all His ways are justice,
A God of truth and without injustice;
Righteous and upright is He.
DEUTERONOMY 32:4

Holiness

Why are some religious leaders, like the Pope and the Dalai Lama, referred to as "his Holiness"? There is no suggestion that these leaders are holy in the sense of being without sin. Instead, it means they have been designated as leaders of their religious movements.

The word *holy* shares its meaning with the word *saint*, a term that the New Testament uses to refer to Christians. Every follower of Christ is a saint. The Bible says every which means we've been set apart by God as "holy ones" for His service.

Thankfully, we don't have to be perfect to be seen as saints in God's eyes. Holiness is a gift from God, a unique calling.

 As He who called you is holy, you also be holy in all your conduct.
1 PETER 1:15

Mercy

Many cities have at least one hospital known as the "mercy" hospital, where no one is turned away. Healthcare is provided regardless of one's ability to pay. Those hospitals "have mercy," so to speak, on everyone who enters their doors.

Christianity is like a mercy hospital. We come to God with empty hands, unable to pay the cost of having our sins forgiven. And we ask God to "have mercy" on us—and He does. He can show mercy because His own Son stepped in and paid the bill for us. How wonderful it is not to be turned away!

God's mercy covers all our sin, all our needs. And it is abundant and without cost.

Therefore the LORD will wait,
that He may be gracious to you;
And therefore He will be exalted,
that He may have mercy on you.
ISAIAH 30:18

Parenting

Parents are the conduits by which the stuff of life is transferred from one generation to the next. It's also the realm in which children and young adults are supposed to learn about God.

The Bible calls God our heavenly Father—a spiritual parent, if you will. And the best way children can learn about God is for their parents to act like Him—especially when it comes to forgiveness. That's a tough one. Children are going to fail, and it's a parent's job to forgive. The more children experience their parents' forgiveness and grace, the more they'll seek out God's forgiveness, both now and as they grow up.

Experience God's compassion and mercy. Pass it on!

 As a father has compassion on his children, so the LORD has compassion on those who fear him.
PSALM 103:13 NIV

God's Forgiveness

The Irish rock star Bono has gained notoriety around the world for something completely outside of his music. He has publicly encouraged world leaders to eradicate the debts of struggling countries who have no means for paying what they owe.

There's a difference between eradicating a debt and forgiving it. To eradicate a debt means it is not paid—it's just taken off the books; a debt that has been forgiven has been paid. The Bible never says our sins were eradicated. Instead, it says they were *forgiven:* the debt was actually paid, though not by us. Jesus paid the debt we had no hope of paying ourselves. God was satisfied and pronounced us "forgiven."

God's great forgiveness is a powerful thing—it gives us hope for now and for eternity. Accept and celebrate that forgiveness.

 For He made Him who knew no sin to be sin for us, that we might become the righteousness of God in Him.
2 CORINTHIANS 5:21

Choices

Advertisers and marketers know that giving consumers too many choices in a product— too many colors, sizes, shapes, or styles—leads to passivity: consumers can't decide, so they simply don't choose. Therefore, marketers limit the choices to products with clear differences between them. Consumers will choose if their choices are made plain.

We like our choices to be made clear in everything, don't we? We don't like fine print, getting the runaround, or doublespeak. Fortunately for us, the Bible is filled with choices that are very clear. We'll never be able to say to God, "Why didn't you make it plain?"

Jesus is the only way to know the Father. It couldn't be any clearer!

 Jesus said to him, "I am the way, the truth, and the life. No one comes to the Father except through Me."
JOHN 14:6

Despair

A twentieth-century French philosopher and author named Albert Camus is widely associated with a worldview of despair. Camus saw the world as absurd and having no purpose; its only goal was death. Any attempt to find purpose beyond biological life is futile under Camus's worldview.

It's not hard to see why Camus was associated with despair, is it? If death is all one has to look forward to in life . . . well, despair makes sense. In the Bible, we find words of Jesus that are, not surprisingly, entirely different from Camus's. Jesus said He came to give us life—life that is abundant. Those are words of hope and not despair.

Live the abundant life today in hope and joy.

 Therefore, having been justified by faith, we have peace with God through our Lord Jesus Christ, through whom also we have access by faith into this grace in which we stand, and rejoice in hope of the glory of God.
ROMANS 5:1–2

Tragedy

Tragedies happen so frequently and so consistently that we almost become immune to them. In the news daily there is some kind of event or other that has the potential to break our hearts and cause us to weep for those affected. And some events are so horrific—tsunamis, terrorist attacks—that we mingle our tears together in corporate pain.

When you weep for yourself or others, what are you thinking? Do tragedies tend to make you bitter, or do they make you better? Bitter is certainly understandable, but better is possible, too. With God's comfort, the Bible says, sadness can be turned to joy.

God is an expert at making stories of triumph out of tragedy. Ask Him for His comfort and grace.

 He heals the brokenhearted
And binds up their wounds.
PSALM 147:3

God's Guidance

A man stopped at a gas station to buy a soda and found a sign on the machine that read: "Sodas three dollars." When he inquired about the steep price, the owner said people ignored the "Out of Order" sign he had on the machine and kept putting their money in anyway, which he then had to return to them. He finally raised the price so high that people stopped trying.

Too often we ignore God's clear directions for living until the price gets so high that we stop. Wouldn't life be better if we read God's book of directions to begin with?

Take the time to study and apply those directions for life. We're promised blessings if we do.

> Show me Your ways, O LORD;
> Teach me Your paths.
> Lead me in Your truth and teach me,
> For You are the God of my salvation;
> On You I wait all the day.
>
> PSALM 25:4–5

Pessimism

In spite of her best efforts, a waitress was unable to cheer up the dejected woman she was serving. When the woman paid her bill, the waitress thanked her and said, "Have a nice day!" The woman snapped, "Sorry, but I've made other plans!"

That's pessimism personified. Some people get out of bed every morning expecting to have a bad day—and they usually do. But the Bible takes a different approach, saying each day is one God has made, in which we should rejoice and be glad (Psalm 118:24).

How did you get out of bed this morning? Thank Him for each day and for all the blessings it may bring.

Let all who seek You rejoice and be glad in You;
And let those who love Your salvation say continually,
"Let God be magnified!"
PSALM 70:4

Balance

You're familiar with the proverb that says, "All work and no play makes Jack a dull boy." Well here's a different take on it: "All work and no play makes Jack the richest guy in the cemetery." And here's the Bible's own view: "What profit is it to a man if he gains the whole world, and loses his own soul?" (Matthew 16:26).

Balance is a lost art in our hectic world. We all need to work diligently, but taking time off from work to relax helps keep everything in perspective.

If you live as a busy, wealthy person, that's fine. Just don't let it be what you're remembered for.

Delight yourself also in the LORD,
And He shall give you the desires of your heart.
PSALM 37:4

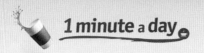

Gossip

Have you ever noticed how often the phrase "It's none of my business" is followed by the word *but?* Human beings find it almost impossible not to tend to other peoples' business. One person said, "I hate to repeat gossip, but what else can I do with it?"

When we listen to or repeat information about another person, we violate their right to privacy. The Bible says there is only one person with the right to know everything about my life, and that is God. And if God tells anyone, it will be because He has my best interests at heart.

If He trusts you to know, He trusts you to pray.

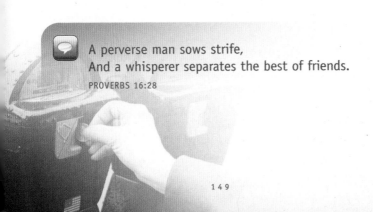

A perverse man sows strife,
And a whisperer separates the best of friends.
PROVERBS 16:28

Christlikeness

A young seminary student was serving as a chaplain in the emergency room of a large charity hospital when a woman was brought in who had tried to take her own life. He did his best to comfort her and after a few minutes, in her agitated state, she looked up and asked, "Are you Jesus?"

Without thinking about it, that young student had fulfilled his life's purpose—to reveal to the world the compassion of Jesus Christ. The Bible says the world will know Christians by how they love others—if their love is like the love of Jesus.

Act in selfless love today and "be Jesus" to someone.

My little children, let us not love in word or in tongue, but in deed and in truth.

1 JOHN 3:18

Paradoxes

We live in a paradoxical world. People live in mobile homes that don't move. We wear sports clothes to work. We wear sweatshirts to relax in. And we eat jumbo shrimp on our working vacations. These paradoxes are humorous, of course, and fun to think about. But some paradoxes can be hard to get used to.

The kingdom of God is filled with paradoxes, too. We give in order to receive; we live by dying; we become great by being a servant; and we find ourselves by losing ourselves in Christ. The more we meditate on these biblical truths, the more at home in God's kingdom we'll be.

Spend time meditating on God's truths and ask Him for help in understanding His ways. He'll be more than happy to answer your prayer for wisdom.

 "For My thoughts are not your thoughts,
Nor are your ways My ways," says the LORD.
ISAIAH 55:8

Authority

When a policeman pulled over a driver for speeding, the man was none too pleased. "Why don't you people get organized?" the driver said. "Yesterday you took away my driver's license and today you want to see it!"

It's easy to find ourselves perturbed with our public officials—especially when we're caught doing something wrong. But the Bible has two simple solutions for this dilemma. First, we should view civil authorities as God's representatives. Second, we should pray regularly for them. I'm always amazed at how hard it is to be mad at someone I'm praying for God to bless.

We are called by God to obey and respect civil authorities. Be a good citizen and bring glory to God.

 Therefore I exhort first of all that supplications, prayers, intercessions, and giving of thanks be made for all men, for kings and all who are in authority, that we may lead a quiet and peaceable life in all godliness and reverence.

1 TIMOTHY 2:1–2

Optimism

A woman in a retirement home was given a party to celebrate her one-hundredth birthday, and a reporter from the local paper showed up to interview her. As he collected information from the woman about her life, he asked whether she had any children. "Not yet!" she replied.

Now that's what I call optimism—a "never-say-never" attitude about life. She must have been familiar with the Bible story about Abraham and Sarah who had their first child when they were around one hundred.

It pays not to give up on God. Faith and hope in Him will keep your eyes on the future in life's impossibilities.

 " 'Ah, Lord GOD! Behold, You have made the heavens and the earth by Your great power and outstretched arm. There is nothing too hard for You.' "
JEREMIAH 32:17

Honesty

See if you don't agree with the following description of an honest person: an honest person is someone with whom you could play checkers over the phone. I like that! They've got the checkerboard in front of them, and you're trusting them to make the moves you dictate over the phone.

Honesty is the currency of the kingdom—it's how we do business together. If we can't trust what we tell each other, the system of human exchange breaks down. The Bible puts it this way: we are to speak the truth in love (Ephesians 4:15).

Even if it's uncomfortable, honesty is always the best policy.

 He who gives a right answer kisses the lips.
PROVERBS 24:26

Values Clarification

A controversial part of the curriculum of many schools is called "values clarification." This teaching says that values are derived from each individual's thoughts and feelings. A popular bumper sticker from a few years back—"If It Feels Good, Do It!"—is an expression of this point of view.

But America's values as a nation weren't rooted in the feelings of the founding fathers. The values they incorporated into our founding documents were drawn from the Bible. And the Bible's values represent God's values.

The best way to clarify the values that have served mankind for centuries is to study them in God's Word. His values should be our values.

 "Therefore you shall lay up these words of mine in your heart and in your soul. . . . You shall teach them to your children, speaking of them when you sit in your house, when you walk by the way, when you lie down, and when you rise up."

DEUTERONOMY 11:18–19

Dr. David Jeremiah is the senior pastor of Shadow Mountain Community Church in El Cajon, California. He is the author of several best-selling books, including *Captured by Grace* and *Signs of Life*. Dr. Jeremiah's popular syndicated Bible-teaching program, Turning Point, is broadcast internationally via radio, TV and the Internet. He and his wife, Donna, live in southern California along with their four children and ten grandchildren.

Endnotes

1 *Notes and Queries* s9-XII: 377.

2 J. R. L. Highfield, *The Private Lives of Albert Einstein* (New York: St. Martin's Press, 1993), 211.

3 Mick Jagger and Keith Richards, "Satisfaction," 1965, www.rollingstone.com/news/story/6595847/i_can't-get-no-satisfaction.

4 Bob Greene. *Notes on the Kitchen Table.* (NY: Doubleday, 1998), 102.

5 John Wooden, *My Personal Best* (New York: McGraw-Hill, 2004), 116.

6 *Merriam-Webster's Collegiate Dictionary,* 11th ed. (Springfield, Massachusetts: Merriam-Webster, Incorporated, 2007), 1143.

7 Sarah Miller Llana, "Why 'Integrity' Was Such a Sought-After Word This Year," *Christian Science Monitor* December 20, 2005, http://www.csmonitor.com/2005/1220/p02s01-ussc.html.

8 *Merriam-Webster's,* 650.

9 Lawrence Jones. "Court Overturns Ban on Prayer in Jesus' Name, Skirts Constitution Question," *The Christian Post* 3 November 2007, http://www.christianpost.com/article/20071103/29942_Court_ Overturns_Ban_on_Prayer in_Jesus%27_Name%2C_Skirts_Constitution_Question.htm.

10 C. S. Lewis, *The Lion, the Witch, and the Wardrobe* (New York: HarperCollins, 1950), 80.

11 Victor Parachin, "God's 911," *Today's Christian* September/October 2000, http://www.christianitytoday.com/tc/2000/005/6.65.html.

12 Joel Garreau, "The Invincible Man: Aubrey de Grey, 44 Going on 1,000, Wants Out of Old Age," *The Washington Post* 31 October 2007, sec. C, p. 1.

13 Robert L. Short, *The Gospel According to Peanuts* (Louisville, KY: Westminster John Knox Press, 2000), 67.

14 Bill Watterson, *The Days are Just Packed* (Kansas City, MO: Andrews and McMeel (Universal Press Syndicate Co., 1993), 36.

15 Elizabeth MacDonald, "Money, Happiness, and the Pursuit of Both," *Forbes.com* 14 February 2006, http://www.forbes.com/2006/02/11/money-happiness-consumption_cz_em_money06_0214pursuit.html.

16 John Greenleaf Whittier, "Maud Muller" in *John Greenleaf Whittier: Selected Poems,* ed. Brenda Wineapple (New York: Literary Classics of the United States, Inc., 2004), 49.

17 Gilda Radner, *It's Always Something* (New York: Simon and Schuster, 1989).

18 *Merriam-Webster's,* 641.

19 Pranay Gupte, "Lunch at The Four Seasons with: Sheri Wilson-Gray," *New York Sun,* 12 December 2005.

20 C.S. Lewis. "Screwtape Letters" in *The Complete C.S. Lewis Signature Classics* (New York:HarperSanFrancisco, 2002), 125.

21 David Callahan. *The Cheating Culture: Why More Americans Are Doing Wrong to Get Ahead* (Harcourt Books, 2004).

22 Troy Goodman, "Do men really listen with just half a brain? Research sheds some light," *CNN.com* 28 November 2000, http://archives.cnn.com/2000/HEALTH/11/28/brain.listening/index.html.

Turning Points
Daily Devotional

Life is a series of decisions and with each decision comes an opportunity for a turning point in our lives. Which direction to go may not always be clear, but God's Word promises to enlighten our ways. *Turning Points* is Dr. Jeremiah's second collection of daily meditations from the Bible that will equip you to live with God's perspective. This topically arranged book of devotions enables you to relate biblical truths to the reality of everyday living— every day of the year!

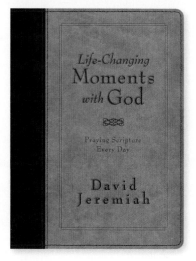

Life-Changing Moments with God
Daily Devotional

No devotional has touched Christians' hearts quite like *Daily Light*. Now this beloved classic is updated for today's reader in *Life-Changing Moments with God* 365-Day Devotional. Featured are Dr. Jeremiah's favorite selections with paraphrased Scripture from the NKJV in first and second person, followed by a short prayer. Readers will draw closer to God's presence and love as they understand clearly that God's Word is personally directed to them.

Find a daily cup
of instant inspiration from
David Jeremiah waiting for you
each morning at home or work.
Log on to www.DavidJeremiah.org
and sign up for Dr. Jeremiah's
daily online e-devotional,
Your Daily Turning Point.